Kendo Guide For Beginners

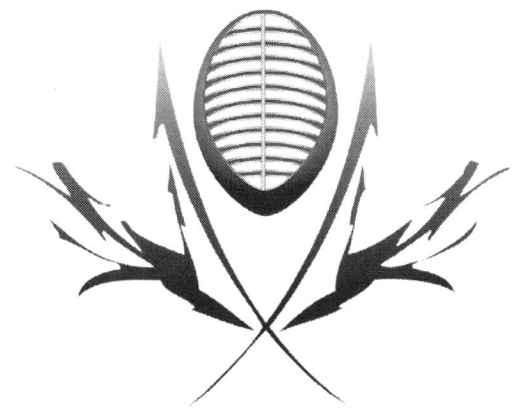

By Masahiro Imafuji

© 2017 by Masahiro Imafuji
All rights reserved.

All Rights Reserved. No part of this publication may be reproduced in any form or by any means, including scanning, photocopying, or otherwise without prior written permission of the copyright holder.

Disclaimer and Terms of Use: The Author and Publisher has strived to be as accurate and complete as possible in the creation of this book, notwithstanding the fact that he does not warrant or represent at any time that the contents within are accurate due to the rapidly changing nature of the Internet. While all attempts have been made to verify information provided in this publication, the Author and Publisher assumes no responsibility for errors, omissions, or contrary interpretation of the subject matter herein. Any perceived slights of specific persons, peoples, or organizations are unintentional. In practical advice books, like anything else in life, there are no guarantees of income made. Readers are cautioned to reply on their own judgment about their individual circumstances to act accordingly. This book is not intended for use as a source of legal, business, accounting or financial advice. All readers are advised to seek services of competent professionals in legal, business, accounting, and finance field.

Cover Design: Andy García (kimochineina.com)

First Printing, 2011
ISBN-13: 978-1463695330
ISBN-10: 1463695330

Printed in the United States of America

ACKNOWLEDGEMENTS

First of all, I would like to thank my family, Elizabeth, and my children, Sophia and Lucas. My wife has patiently helped and supported me with my activities for the *kendo* community. My children are the source of my energy. Without their smiles and cheerful voices, it would have been lot tougher to reach where I am now.

I would like to give my special thanks to Young Park *sensei* who is the *dōjō* owner and let me use the *dōjō* for the photo shooting. I appreciate Ramón Carrera who volunteered to take these photos with his own camera and equipment and Joyce Lee who helped as his assistant. And I would like to thank my *kendo* mates; the students at Indianapolis Kendo Club, especially Brian Dirk, Andrew Schultz, Steve Black, Mark Ritter who have been the strong members of the club, and Gotokukan Imafuji *Dojo* members. They constantly encourage me to teach and learn *kendo* together; the former and current members of Sei Tou Ken Yu Kai in Christchurch, New Zealand, especially Karl Hitchcock, Gordon Evans, Hamish Robison, Ben Miskin, Nic Ferra, the Satos and Blake Bennett, my Kiwi little brother, who constantly influences my teaching methods with his unique instruction approaches; the former and current Sei Shin Ken Yu Kai and Guatemala Kendo Association in Guatemala, especially the late Enzo Marsicovetere, Carlos Campos, Herman Westphal, Arkel Marsicovetere, Pedro Velásquez, Elías Abraham who helped me go through cultural differences; Alex Bennett, the editor-in-chief of Kendo World Magazine and my Kiwi older brother, who checked this book and gave me advice to make it better. And Hajime Sugawara *sensei* who took the photos of the cover page of the book.

There are financial supporters too; David, Alberto Ferrer, Melvin Nguyen, Roman Nobbe, Beowulf, Mark Bamberry, Paul Gilmore, Lance Lee Carder, Troy Girard, makotoevo, Gabriela Meda, Raymond Rodriguez, Saku Putkonen, Michael Flores, Stefan Eisenmann, Sung Lee, Larry Guillot, John Emory, Tom Pearce, Sebastián López Bosque, Cristiano Baptista, Duc-Thai Hoang, Juna, Lander Mazon, Marcer Maxime, Christoph Lintermanns, Carlos Matutes, Alex Kim, Kenneth Burke, Michael Zappe, Hilda Sanchez, Patrick Kamuela Hicks, Come Train or Come Shine, Ryan Vallance, Nakamura Marten, Min Chih Wang, Steve Black, Renee Shaffer, Tyler Rice, Seyi Ogunyemi, Anne Snair, Thomas Jenney, Eric S Adair, KendoGirl.com, Khamphou Boutdavong, Mateusz Malisiewicz, Steve McKenzie, Ramon Carrera, Garcia Perez Cesareo, Hrishikesh Juvale, Julius Gyula Hargitai, UberMx, William Coble, Louis-xavier Dauguet, Kobi Levi, Joseph A. Clark, Valerie Lofthouse, Jimmy Broyles, Wara Cascajares, Andrew Schultz, Scott Lewis, Julien Loze, Joe Collazo, Nicholas Eftimiades, Raul G Rodriguez, Claudia Doppioslash, Kate Duffus, Neil Andrews, Konrad Faltyn, Christopher Paul, Sergio Velasquez, Joe Black, Lander Mazon, Shane Robinson, Ming Foong Lam, John Bradford, MSgt Rick Newman, Stelios, John Tye, Ahmed Gaballa, FoongNee Lam, Nurayuni Amirah, Saku Putkonen, Grady Gillis, Bruce alter, Aleksander Wirecki, Matthew Vetrini, David St John, Leandro de Sousa, Kentaro Makino, Wendy Vermeulen from Patreon.Com. Thanks to them I can keep creating the *kendo* content with videos, podcasts and articles, and purchase equipment that is necessary to create the content.

Every person whom I have interacted with is my reason to have this book finished. I really appreciate the encouraging messages through emails and social networks.

And last but not least I would like to thank and dedicate this *Kendo Guide for Beginners* to the following men who taught me *kendo* and who greatly influenced my life:

The late Juichi TSURUMARU *sensei* (9-*dan*),

The main instructor when I started *kendo*.
The instructions here are based on his methods.

The late Keisuke MURAYAMA *sensei* (8-*dan*),

(By courtesy of Kinji Murayama *sensei*)
The then second main instructor and All Japan 8-dan Champion.
He showed me the way and admired what I did for *kendo* in different countries.

Masayoshi MIYAZAKI *sensei* (7-*dan*),

My direct *kendo* master and great influencer to my life.
I am still learning a lot from him.

The late Enzo Marsicovetere (3-dan)

A great kendoist and one of my best friends from Guatemala.
Without him, I couldn't have achieved anything in Guatemala.

And my late father, Shigesaburō IMAFUJI (5-*dan*)

A great father, influencer and *kendo* mate of mine.
He would be super happy about the book.

KENDO FOR LIFE, LLC

- **Watch with This Book: The Basics at YouTube Channel:** https://www.youtube.com/user/dojo2go
  - **Kendo Basics I:** https://www.youtube.com/playlist?list=PLmdvM8fwuCxhn8XJH49FEWwjiaqrt9AmJ
  - **Kendo Basics II:** https://www.youtube.com/playlist?list=PLmdvM8fwuCxg165MaeTChmrWHJj4O77y
  - **Kendo Basics III:** https://www.youtube.com/playlist?list=PLmdvM8fwuCxjuQ1lPtPNojqwB8LoFW_WA

- **Interview with Alex Bennett:** Interview with Alex Bennett who passed 7-*dan* exam at his first attempt. https://youtu.be/IpbAaJ-r9vU
- **Kendo-Guide.Com Newsletter:** Get Updates from Kendo-Guide.Com. Free email newsletter published by Kendo For Life, LLC. http://www.kendo-guide.com/why_subscribe.html
- **Facebook Page:** https://www.facebook.com/KendoGuideCom/

CONTENTS

	Editorial Note	i
1	Kendō Guide for Beginners	1
2	Learning Kendō: The Big Picture	3
3	Kendō Equipment: General Information	5
4	Normal Training Procedure	9
5	Etiquette/Manners	12
6	Kendō Terminology	17
7	Kendō Basics by Kendō Guide for Beginners	20
8	How to Sit in Seiza	22
9	How to Bow in the Standing and Sitting Position	24
10	Mokusō Breathing: Quiet but Powerful	26
11	Shizentai	**28**
12	Tai-tō	30
13	Chūdan	33
14	How to Hold the Shinai Properly	**36**
15	Basic Kendō Footwork	41
16	Jōge-buri Cuts	48
17	Men Strike: Basic Men Training for Beginners	56
18	Kote Strike: Basic Kote-uchi	61

19	Dō Strike: Basic Dō-uchi	65
20	Zenshin-kōtai Shō-men Strike	69
21	Niho-zenshin Niho-kōtai Men Strike	73
22	Kote-men Strike: Basic Kote-men Strike in Suburi	76
23	Kote-dō Strike: Basic Kote-dō Strike in Suburi	80
24	Sayū-men: The Core Movement of Kirikaeshi	83
25	First Time Fumikomi? Learn it Step by Step	85
26	Haya-suburi: No Different from Other Suburi	86

EDITORIAL NOTE

Japanese words are written in italics. This book uses macrons ("ō" and "ū") to represent elongated pronunciation of vowels, except in titles of organizations names where they are not utilized.

1. KENDŌ GUIDE FOR BEGINNERS

This book is for people who

- Want to learn *kendō* but have no access to a *dōjō* (*kendō* training hall), or
- Want to revise what they have already learnt at their *dōjō*.

This book only covers the fundamental *kendō* movements, terms, etiquette and manners.

Many people have asked me this question: **Can you learn *kendō* on your own?**

This is one of the frequently asked questions at the Kendo-Guide.Com website, and my answer is an emphatic NO. No one can learn *kendō* alone. We need to have at least one training partner, and we need a good teacher to guide us, and to put us back on the right track when we take a wrong turn.

However, there are many people out there who do not have easy access to a place where they can learn *kendō* properly. There are many cities and regions with no *dōjō*, and finding a good *kendō* instructor can be very difficult. It is also true that are few **GOOD** *kendō* resources out there to aid people in their study. So what can we do to help people who want to learn *kendō* but do not have access to a *dōjō*?

- Do we ignore them?
- Do we just tell them to wait until a *dōjō* opens in their city?
- Do we tell them to earn a lot of money so they can travel to a *dōjō* 200 miles away on a regular basis?
- Do we just let them learn *kendō* from untrustworthy *kendō* resources?

It is heart-breaking to see potential kendoists brimming with enthusiasm and passion falling in with the wrong crowd and learning a dubious version of *kendō* because they do not know any better. *Kendō* is not something that just anyone can teach after a couple of years of taking lessons. It has to be studied intensively for many years under the auspices of qualified and experienced instructors before one gains enough knowledge to teach. If you are looking for an instructor, you must take careful note of his or her credentials, and what it is that they are teaching.

This book outlines traditional *kendō* learning methods for beginners. If you study the movements and theories thoroughly here, you will gain an understanding of *kendō* basics to put you in good stead when you have the opportunity to study under a qualified and dependable instructor.

Everybody needs constant input from instructors regardless of what they are studying. If you do not have a *dōjō* to go to, you will miss out on this crucial aspect of learning, and will develop all sorts of bad, hard-to-fix habits. Following the instructions in this book will at least help you recognize what "authentic" *kendō* is, as opposed to the "backyard ninja" who professes to teach *kendō*.

This book is not meant to be a "teach yourself" primer, but is simply a guide to help you to understand the most basic movements and etiquette. It should be used as supplementary material to training in a *dōjō*, even if it is a long way from where you live. It is my hope that this book will prepare you for learning *kendō* in a proper *dōjō* or club, nothing more.

The importance of the basics

The basics (*kihon*) is the most important thing in *kendō*. We always have to come back to the basics regardless of what grade we hold. Even **9-*dan*** teachers such as the late Tsurumaru-sensei, who I was lucky to study under as a child, always emphasised the importance of reviewing the basics.

Many want to learn *kendō* because they are attracted to the idea of doing "cool stuff" with a sword. That is fine, so long as you remember that you will not be able to do anything without thoroughly learning *kihon* first. Still, many students are impatient, and want to skip the *kihon* to get straight into more advanced techniques. Most of them end up quitting.

The reason why they quit is simple. If you do not learn *kihon* properly, you will have no foundation to build on. You may be able to learn a few "tricks" quickly, and win a few matches, but your *kendō* will start to crumble. Those who actually took the time to learn *kihon* will eventually take you apart. Not learning *kihon* properly will cause your *kendō* demise.

For sure, *kendō* is more enjoyable when you have an extensive repertoire of techniques up your sleeve, and it is satisfying to learn something new. But be warned, all of the advanced techniques are built on *kihon*, and whether you like it or not, enduring the hard grind to master the 'boring basics' is the only way you will be able to advance in *kendō*.

Take *kihon* seriously, and learn it well; your *kendō* career will be much more enjoyable in the long run, and you will be able to practice throughout your life with a solid foundation.

2. LEARNING KENDŌ: THE BIG PICTURE

Kendō is hard to learn. If you have already studied *kendō*, you will have already noticed that progress is usually slow. Before we get into how we should learn *kendō*, I would like to tell you how *kendō* is studied in Japan.

Age: Most people outside of Japan start *kendō* in their adulthood, whereas the Japanese typically start *kendō* at an early age. I started *kendō* at the age of 7. Some start even younger. What does this mean in the grand scheme of things? I do not wish to imply that you cannot learn *kendō* if you do not start it as a child. What I am saying is that you should not get frustrated because you cannot pick it up as quickly as some other martial art.

Children learn very quickly, and they are not afraid of making mistakes. Children will learn by trial and error, and do not usually get as frustrated with failure as adults are apt to. They enjoy the process of making mistakes and improving their skills. Through my experiences in instructing *kendō*, adults tend to get discouraged when they cannot see their own progress straight away. Frustration leads to more mistakes. In turn that makes them more perturbed, and eventually they think that *kendō* is not right for them.

That is an unfortunate, but all-to-common conclusion. *Kendō* involves many movements that will be totally unfamiliar to the novice. It is normal not to be able to execute them properly after only a few tries. Please don't feel that *kendō* is not for you, or that you are a slow learner. If you feel this way, then you may find the following video helpful: "How To Learn The *Kendō* Movements More Easily And Quickly".[1]

Environment: Learning by watching is a very important process in *kendō*. How does this affect those who live outside Japan? Children in Japan go to a *dōjō* where there are typically several experienced instructors who are usually 6-*dan* or above. They also have the luxury of having plenty of other students as their seniors or *sempai*.[2] From the very beginning, children in Japan are surrounded by quality kendoists who serve as their role models. They learn not only from direct instruction, but also by watching other practitioners.

Children learning *kendō* in Japan also have problems with learning *kendō* movements, but they can learn through osmosis, by being in a *dōjō* with experienced practitioners. People learning outside Japan do not have such a conducive learning environment. Many *dōjō* outside Japan do not even have instructors. Having no experienced instructors means that there are no people to observe and learn from leading to bad habits, inappropriate equipment, and so on. This is a big problem. Without good models for *kendō* movement, the learning process is very slow, and novices think that they are not progressing. They quit before they experience the real joys of *kendō*.

Information: People who wish to learn *kendō* and end up going to a *dōjō* that does not teach correctly, are not actually learning *kendō*. Sadly, these people do not know they are learning incorrect forms. I am certainly not trying to discourage you from learning *kendō*, but tell you how important it is for you to learn *kendō* properly from the outset. If you do not have good resources such as *dōjō* and *sensei* available, don't waste your time searching the Internet to get started. Through this small book, I want to assist you with learning correct basics so that when you begin at a *dōjō*, you will have a head start. With solid basics, you can learn techniques easily, and you will spend less time correcting bad habits.

It takes a long time to understand what is actually going on in *kendō*. I do not know your age, what environment you are in, or what kind of information you have. But I know this —

---

[1] http://www.kendo-guide.com/How-to-Learn-Kendo-Movements-More-Easily-and-Quickly.html

[2] Sempai means those who have done *kendō* longer.

The longer you do *kendō*, the more you will enjoy it, and the more profound your knowledge will become

You will be awestruck at old people can dominate young people in *kendō*. I want you to experience that too. If you have not tried to search *dōjō* in your area, you can try the Kendo-Guide.Com *dōjō* search.[3] Can you tell if the instructor is the real deal or not? Read some tips at "How Can You Tell if an Instructor is Good or Not?"[4]

---

[3] http://www.kendo-guide.com/kendo_dojo_search.html

[4] Column: How Can You Tell If an Instructor is Good or Not?, p.40

3. KENDŌ EQUIPMENT: GENERAL INFORMATION

If you decide to take up *kendo*, you will need equipment. Here is what you will need:

- Wooden sword or *bokutō* (*bokken*)
- Bamboo sword or *shinai*
- Training wear (top and bottom), and later on,
- A set of armour or *bōgu*

The top part of the training wear is called *keikogi* and the bottom the *hakama*. At the very beginning you will not need all the equipment. A **shinai** or **bokutō** will suffice. Training wear is also good to have from the outset. In any case, follow the instructions of your club leader with regards to necessary equipment.

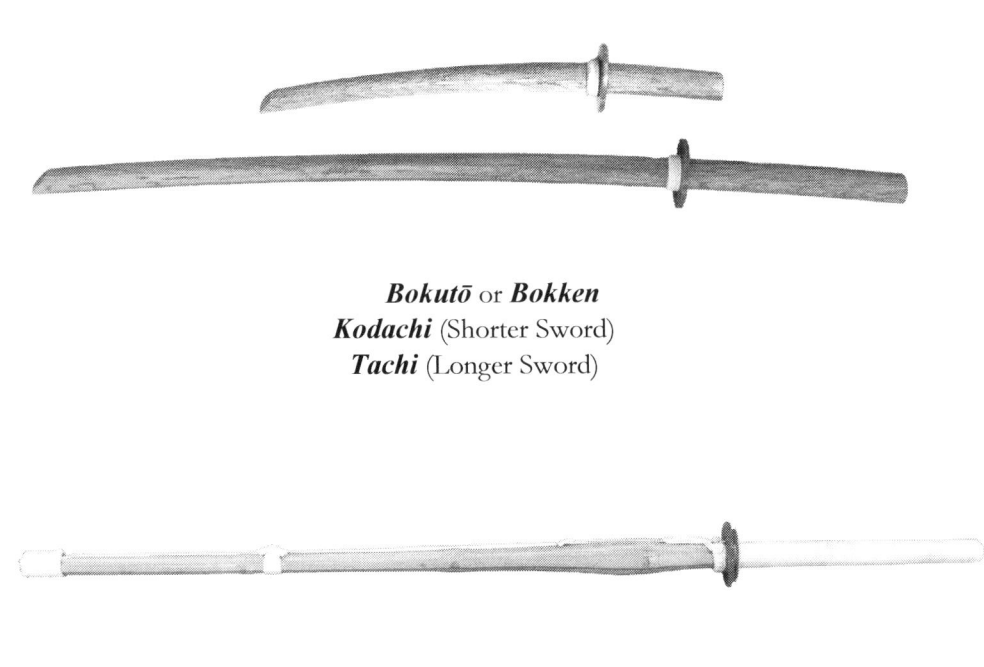

Bokutō or **Bokken**
Kodachi (Shorter Sword)
Tachi (Longer Sword)

Shinai

Traditionally *keikogi* and *hakama* should be worn in the *dōjō* so that we can develop the correct mind-set. I think that you only need **bokutō** to start with, and then gradually purchase *keikogi*, *hakama*, and *shinai*. The reason is that it can be a little pricey to start with. If you are happy to buy everything from the outset, then that is also okay. You will need a *shinai* when you start working with a partner because we do not want to hit anything with *bokutō*!

Choosing a *Shinai*

It's economical to know how to choose a *shinai* that will not break easily. Besides, when you become more advanced, you will work out a preference for *shinai* that suit your style based on factors such as the centre of balance. In any case, this is an acquired skill that you do not have to worry about at the novice stage.

** Maintaining your *Shinai* **

Kendō is the safest martial art as long as we take good care of our *shinai*. If your *shinai* is in bad shape, i.e. splintered, there is a possibility that you will **hurt** your training partner.

- ※ Knowing how to maintain your *shinai* is vital for you and your partner.[5]
- ※ Knowing how to make *shinai* adjustments is useful when you need to make a *shinai* shorter.[6]

Keikogi & *Hakama* (top and bottom)

You do not have to be too concerned about quality of the uniform at the start of your *kendō* career. Just be careful with martial arts shops that sell peculiar keikogi and *hakama*. Since *kendō* is not particularly well-known, people don't know what *keikogi* and *hakama* should look like. That is why you should be careful when buying gear off the Internet.

Don't go for the cheapest, but rather, the most **"REASONABLE"** price. If you don't know where to buy equipment, the following page will help you choose which site to use: *Kendō* Equipment Shop: Buying *Kendō* Stuff Online[7].

Navy Blue or White *Keikogi* and *Hakama*?

Top: Keikogi

Bottoms: Hakama

Kendō uniform seems less important than *bōgu*, but you can encounter some problems. Stick to **tradition** and what the **majority** wear. That is the safest way when you start anything new. I advise you buy a navy blue *keikogi* and *hakama*, not white. If you wear navy blue *keikogi* and *hakama*, you will blend in. However, if you wear white some people may not like the way you look. White *keikogi* and *hakama* are often seen as for "special" occasions. Some people even say that white is the best because we can see right away when the gear gets dirty. Others think that white *keikogi* and *hakama* are only for females, but this is not true either. Whatever the arguments for and against wearing white, you are best advised to make that decision when you actually know what you are doing. Beginners should stick with blue.

When I was young child, I started training with a *keikogi* with a criss-cross pattern on it called "*musashi*". Stay away from this too if you are an adult. I have never seen Japanese adults wearing a *keikogi* with the *musashi* pattern. Kids up to 10 years old can still wear a *keikogi* with the *musashi* pattern, but after that it becomes a tad embarrassing.

Cotton versus Polyester

Nowadays, there are *keikogi* made from the same polyester as normal athletic training wear as opposed to cotton. These modern *keikogi* are popular in Japan, especially during the hot summers. However, kendoists traditionally wear cotton *keikogi* and *hakama* which fade very quickly from washing. It is OK to wear colour-faded *keikogi* and *hakama* at training, but not at tournaments or promotion examinations as it is looked upon as being a little untidy. Elegance and tidiness is very important.

---

[5] http://www.kendo-guide.com/shinai_maintenance.html

[6] http://www.kendo-guide.com/shinai_adjustment.html

[7] http://www.kendo-guide.com/kendo-equipment-shop.html

Cotton is pricey, so I suggest buying polyester, especially at the beginning. In *kendō* we usually call this type of *hakama* TETRON. Most *kendō* shops have uniforms (the top and bottoms) for beginners; *Kendō* Equipment Shop: Buying *Kendō* Stuff Online.[7]

When Not to Wear Polyester *Keikogi* and *Hakama*

Kendoists who hold the 3-*dan* and above can also wear polyester, but usually do not. It would be akin to going to a formal party in a T-shirt and jeans.

If you hold a *dan* grade, avoid wearing polyester *keikogi* and *hakama* at:

- Tournaments

- Examination

- When training at a different *dojo*, and

- When you host a training session with other *dojo*.

The following is a video shows how to put on *keikogi* and *hakama*: "How To Put Keikogi And Hakama On In *Kendō*".[8]

Kendō Armour or *Bōgu*

We call a set of armour *bōgu* in Japanese. *Bōgu* means "protective equipment". *Kendō* equipment includes a mask (*men*), gauntlets (*kote*), torso protector (*dō*), and lower-body (*tare*). Needless to say, each piece of the equipment is important to protect the body well. However, at the beginning of your *kendō* career, you do not need to splash out on a set for US$5,000. We usually move on to better sets of *bōgu* as we become more skilled and higher in rank. For example, you avoid buying a shiny *dō* with fancy patters on it. It might look nifty, but it is not for beginners. What is important when buying your first set of *bōgu* is the size? It shouldn't be too big, or too small. The size has to be right for you. Every *bōgu* shop will tell you how to measure properly (or at least they should), so when you order your *kendō* equipment be sure to follow their instructions. If you don't know how, you should always ask. If you don't know any good *kendō* shops see some useful reviews here.[9]

---

[8] http://youtube/EsnHqymFK9M

[9] http://www.kendo-guide.com/kendo-shop-review.html

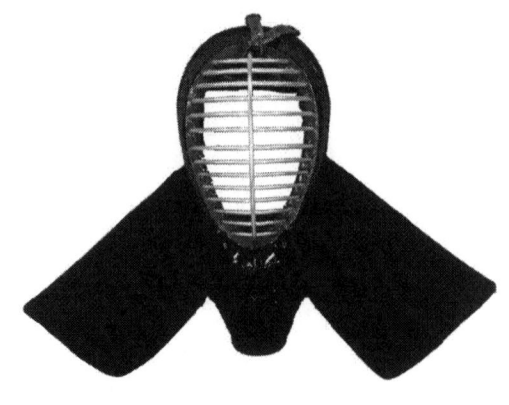 *Men*

 *Kote*

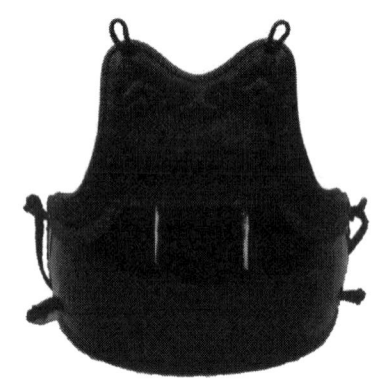 *Dō*

 *Tare*

A Set of *Bōgu*

4. NORMAL TRAINING PROCEDURE

The following is an outline for general *kendō* training procedures. There are also some articles on etiquette/manners in the *dōjō* below.

Begin with a Bow and End with a Bow

As it is said in all *budō* (the martial ways), we start and finish with a bow. Traditional *dōjō* often have a little shrine or altar to protect the practitioners. We bow when entering and leaving the *dōjō* as a show of respect and appreciation to our training venue. Another important function in this bow it is the point when we change our mind-set before and after training. Once we step into a *dōjō*, we are no longer in our "normal world". We are in a place where we train to become better at our art, and by virtue of this, a better person. When we leave the *dōjō*, we bow again. This is to show respect to the *dōjō* we have just used. We can now go back to our normal lives, but with the knowledge that we have learned something from the training.

The following is an outline for a typical training menu:

Line-up

***Mokusō* (meditation)**

Bow to the *shōmen* (altar or front of the *dōjō*), *sensei*, and each other

Training commences

Training ends

Mokusō

Bow to the *sensei*, *shōmen*, and each other

Final talk from the *sensei*

Line-up

Line up in a straight line. There is typically a leader or captain who gives the order to line up. Make sure to place your equipment neatly on the floor.

Mokusō

Usually we will be seated in *seiza* when it is time to begin. When the command for *mokusō* is given, lightly close your eyes, place your left hand on top of your right with the palms facing up, and make a circle with the thumbs. Breathe in through your nose, hold for a few seconds, then breathe out through your mouth. (A more detailed explanation will be given later.) When you hear "*yame*", open your eyes and gently place your hands back on your thighs.

Bow to the *shōmen*, *sensei*, and each other

The *shōmen* is at the front of the *dōjō*. Traditionally, there is a little shrine or scroll on the front wall of the *dōjō* which is bowed to as a sign of appreciation and respect.

Training commences

If you train in *bōgu* (armour), your leader will give the command to put your *men* (mask) on. Otherwise, wait in *seiza* until the others have put on their *men* unless instructed otherwise.

During the training

Follow any instructions given by the leader or instructor. Make sure you bow to your training partners before and after each bout.

Training ends

Everybody lines up again in a straight line at the end of training. Kneel down in *seiza*, and then remove your *men* with the command "*Men wo tore* (or *Men tore*)". Depending on the *dōjō*, you may have to step forward from where your equipment is and line up, or you just stay where you are.

Mokusō

Breathe in through your nose and out through your mouth. Think about how your training went, and what you should have done. It is a good time to reflect on how you can do better in the next training.

Bow to the *sensei*, *shōmen*, and each other

Pay attention to the reverse order. At the beginning of training, we bow to *shōmen* first, but at the end we start by bowing to the *sensei*.

A final talk from the *sensei*

You may be given a small speech from your *sensei* or *sempai* about the training. At this point, do not start taking off your *bōgu*. Stay still in *seiza*, and listen to what they have to say. They will tell you when it is okay to go. Starting to pack up your equipment while your *sensei* is talking is considered very rude.

COLUMN: COMMON INJURIES

Since there is no actual physical contact in *kendō* such as punching and kicking, few people get seriously injured during training or tournaments. However, there are some common injuries which are mainly caused by repetitious movements. The common injuries in *kendō* are listed below. The serious ones can be prevented by doing a good warm-up and stretching before training.

- **Snapping of the Achilles tendon:** As the left leg is used to kick-off and jump forwards, snapping the left Achilles tendon is probably the most serious injury in kendo. (I snapped mine once).

- **Carpal tunnel syndrome**: Because we must use our hands and wrists to swing the *shinai* repeatedly, some people tend to develop carpal tunnel syndrome through repetitive strain.

- **Back pain**: If you try to straighten your back too much, you may develop pain in the lower-back area.

- **Blisters**: Everybody gets blisters! The common places are left hand and soles of the feet. Please refer to "Blister Treatment in Kendō" at Kendo-Guide.Com.[10]

I dislocated my left shoulder too, but fortunately this is not so common.

How can injuries be avoided?

The secret is to not overdo it! If you are blessed with superior athletic ability, then go ahead and train hard as you can. However, if you feel pain somewhere, REST. Go see a doctor. Fix it before it's too late. The reason why I kept hurting myself is because I never took time off training to heal, even after I snapped my Achilles tendon. Of course, I could not move, but I still tried to keep going. In retrospect, this was a very stupid thing to do… When I dislocated my left shoulder, it hurt a lot, but still I kept training. The next day, I could not move my left arm at all, and twenty years later, I needed to have surgery. If you feel pain, it is because you are either injured, or you are doing something wrong. Step back and ask yourself why you are in pain. Ask your teachers why you would be feeling pain. Self-awareness is the key to prevent and recover from injury.

---

[10] http://www.kendo-guide.com/blister_treatment.html

5. ETIQUETTE/MANNERS

Kendō is more than just a matter of hitting other people with a stick. In 1975, the All Japan Kendo Federation announced the official "Concept of Kendo" and its purpose.

The Concept of Kendo

The concept of *kendō* is to discipline the human character through the application of the principles of the *katana* (sword).

The Purpose of Practicing Kendo

To mold the mind and body,

To cultivate a vigorous spirit,

And through correct and rigid training,

To strive for improvement in the art of *Kendō*,

To hold in esteem human courtesy and honor,

To associate with others with sincerity,

And to forever pursue the cultivation of oneself.

This will make one be able:

To love his/her country and society,

To contribute to the development of culture

And to promote peace and prosperity among all peoples.

(The Concept of *Kendō* was established by All Japan Kendo Federation in 1975.)

This should be understood by all *kendō* practitioners. *Kendō* that lacks manners or respect is simply violence.

The Meaning of Dōjō

The *dōjō* is a place for training in the martial arts. The following definitions of *dōjō* are from a dictionary:

- **A place under a *bo* tree where it is said that Sakyamuni (Buddha) attained spiritual enlightenment.**
- **A place Buddhist monks practice Buddhism such as a temple.**
- **A place where a group of people stay mainly to discipline themselves.**

Clearly, *dōjō* means more than just a training place. It has far more spiritual significance attached to it than a gym for playing sports. Once you join a *dōjō*, you have to be ready to train your body and mind, and be prepared to discipline yourself.

Rules of the dōjō

How do we line up? Do you know where you should sit in your *dōjō*? If you do *kendo*, you need to know where you should sit without having to be told. *Kamiza* is for high ranks and *shimoza* for lower ranks. The *kanji* (Japanese characters) for *kamiza* means "upper seat", and "lower seat" for *shimoza*. Once you know where high ranks should sit, it is easy to figure out where you should be in relation to them. The positioning of the main entrance to the *dōjō* plays an important role in working out where the *kamiza* is located — it should be furthest from the main entrance of the *dōjō*. The *shomen* (front) should be across the *dōjō* from the entrance.

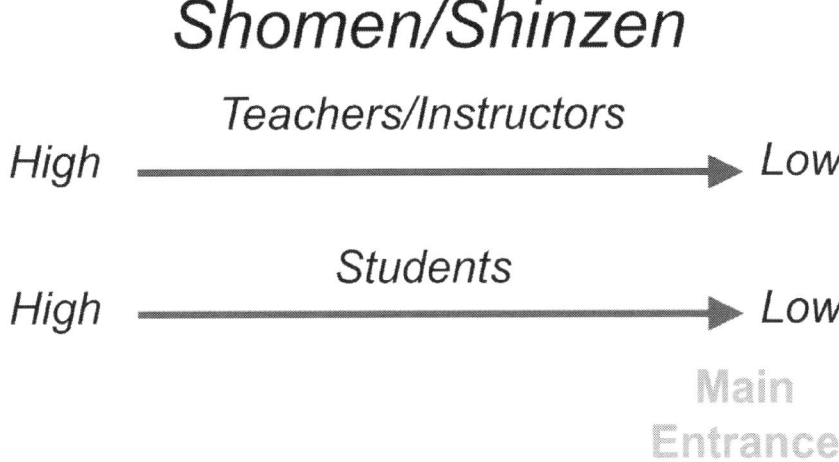

In the illustration above, the main entrance of the *dōjō* is located at the bottom-right. In this case, the higher grade holders should be on the left side of the *dōjō*. The higher you are, the further you are from the entrance.

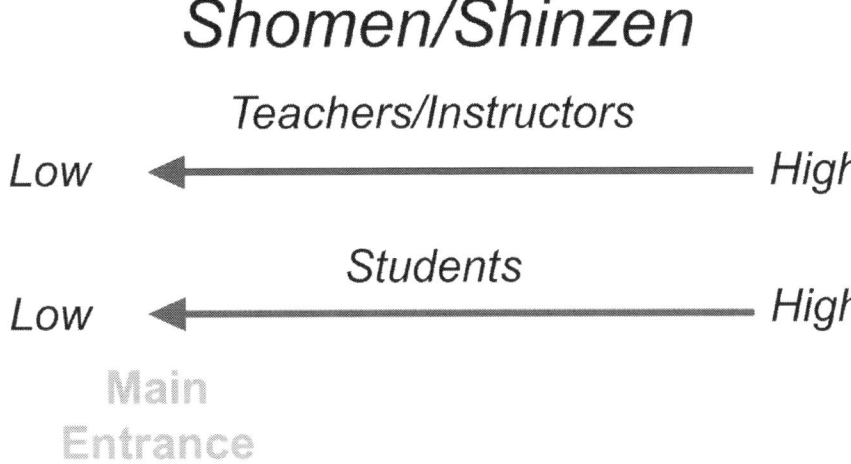

If the main entrance is at the bottom left as illustrated above, the higher ranked teachers and students should be on the right hand side of the *dōjō*. The *shomen* should be the opposite side from the main entrance.

If the main entrance is in the middle, or somewhere difficult to judge, the higher side should be to the right.

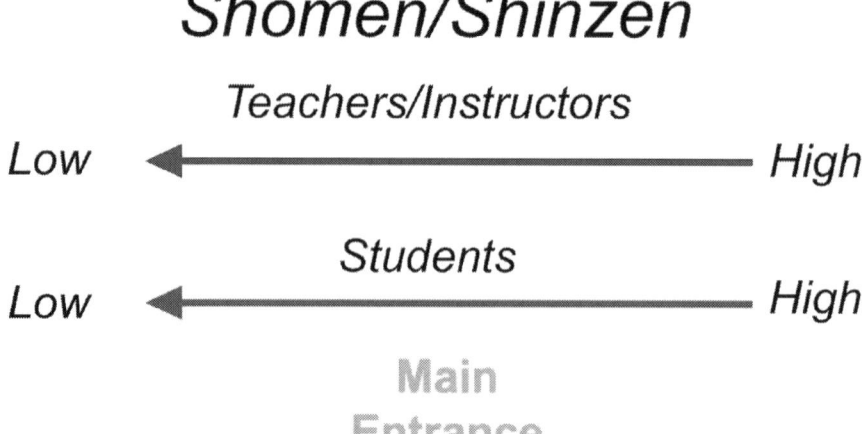

The reason why the higher-ranked people traditionally sit at the *kamiza* away from the main entrance is to avoid attacks from enemies. The lower class or ranks of samurai would sit close to the main entrance to defend their seniors. While the lower warriors were warding off an attack, the seniors could make an escape and prepare for the ensuing battle.

Japanese society still uses this concept to decide seating positions in banquets. If you have a chance to visit Japan, watch carefully how people decide where to sit. For example, when you visit a friend's home, as the guest you will be seated at the *kamiza* of the room, away from the main entrance. However, if you visit a *dōjō* in Japan, as a guest you should never go and sit at the *kamiza* unless invited to do so. You will offend the *dōjō* members, and judged as a person with no manners. That is the last thing you want to do at a *dōjō* – being taught a lesson in manners is never nice…

<u>Before you enter the dōjō</u>

- Take off your shoes
- Bow and enter

Inside the *dōjō*, be sure not to do the following:

- Fail to bow when walking in and out
- Wear a coat or jacket
- Wear a cap or hat
- Sit down with your legs stretched out
- Sit with one or both knees up
- Lay down on the floor
- Eat or drink (except on special occasions)

The *dōjō* is a special place where we separate ourselves from our ordinary life. The *dōjō* is not somewhere to relax. It is not a living room.

Why we don't do certain things in the dōjō

- **Not bowing when entering and leaving**

Stop at the entrance and bow. It shows respect to the *dōjō* and its members. It also puts you in the right frame of mind for training. You must bow every time when you come in and out of the *dōjō*.

- **Wearing a coat or jacket**
- **Wearing a cap or hat**

Traditionally speaking, jackets and hats should never be worn in the *dōjō*. Recently, many young Japanese do not follow these protocols anymore because they don't know the reasoning behind it. In Japan, we take off our shoes when we go into a building such as a house or *dōjō*. Nowadays, many schools let their students wear shoes in class, but when I was at school, we always had to take our shoes off before entering school buildings. In my upbringing, shoes were for outside, as were jackets and caps. It was considered odd to wear them inside when they were not needed. They were originally designed for protecting you from the elements, so why wear them inside?

I imagine it is the same in some other countries as well. When I lived in Guatemala, I saw many people taking off their hats when entering a church as a sign of respect. Etiquette in the *dōjō* is not so different from other sacred places.

- **Sitting down with legs stretched out**
- **Sitting with one or both knees up**
- **Laying down on the floor**

There are only two ways of sitting in a *dōjō*: *seiza* or *agura* (crossing legs). No other ways are acceptable. People with knee problems should sit in a way that is comfortable, but I suggest you talk to your *sensei* if you have a problem with *seiza* or *agura*. In no circumstances should you lie down in the *dōjō*.

- **Eating and drinking**

In general, drinking water during training is now acceptable practice, although it was strictly prohibited when I was younger. If you walk into a *dōjō* chewing gum or eating, you may find yourself in big trouble. Would you go to battle while you were munching on food? There are exceptions though. When we have special events at the *dōjō*, then you may eat and drink as appropriate. I still remember that we used to have meals with *sensei*, students and guests at the *dōjō* when we had special events.

The meaning of "DŌ"

The "*dō*" in *ken-dō*, *ju-dō*, *kyū-dō* and so on means the "Way". *Kendō* is the way of the sword, *judō* is the way of gentleness, and *kyūdō* is the way of the bow. We use "*dō*" for non-martial arts, too. *Shodō* is the way of writing (calligraphy), *sadō* is the way of tea making (tea ceremony), and *kadō* is the way of flower arrangement. Japanese see these activities as Ways to be pursued over a lifetime. They are not intended as entertainment, but contain many teachings which help us to see ourselves objectively in order to improve as a human beings.

Strictly speaking, *budō* should be translated as "martial way", rather than "martial arts". The way is "to pursue whatever we are learning through our lives in order to improve ourselves, and contribute to society by becoming a better person." *Budō*, when translated as "martial art", is often interpreted as techniques to defeat others. This is only one aspect of *budō*. Ideally, it is a way of self-development through training in martial techniques. Some use brushes and pieces of paper for their self-development through calligraphy (*shodō*). Some study tea for the same purpose (*sadō*). We have chosen the way of the sword.

COLUMN: IS KENDŌ A GOOD FORM OF EXERCISE?

There are many people who start *kendō* to maintain fitness. A person once asked me through the Kendo-Guide.Com Q&A section[11] whether or not *kendō* was a good form of exercise. He wanted to know if he could build muscle, and if it would be a good way to keep fit. The answer is yes. *Kendō* is good exercise, and goes a long way to improve physical strength and stamina. However, if you want big muscles like bodybuilders, then *kendō* is probably not for you.

Kendō is both aerobic and anaerobic. Many people think that *kendō* is mostly spiritual, or emphasizes mental aspects, but we train physically hard as well. Actually, some people find the training in *kendō* to be very exhausting even though they think they are fit. (See one of the comments made by Blake Bennett for "How to increase stamina for kendo"[12].) It is not because *kendō* is better exercise than other sports, but it is different. My advice is to take it easy at the start.

Many beginners find it difficult to perform simple footwork exercises at the beginning. The footwork itself is quite simple, but you will need to practice a lot to become proficient. Because it is simple, beginners tend to overdo footwork training and get tired very quickly, and end up with all sorts of aches and pains. Remember, your body has to become accustomed to the movements. Learn to tread water before you swim, otherwise you might find yourself sinking.

---

[11] http://www.kendo-guide.com/kendo_q_a.html

[12] http://www.kendo-guide.com/how-to-increase-my-stamina-for-kendo.html

6. KENDŌ TERMINOLOGY

Kendō terms are in Japanese. If you are familiar with the Japanese language, then you will have less trouble. If you do not know anything about Japanese, you will learn but it may be confusing at the start. The following is a list of the most common terms that you will need to know for a general *kendō* training session.

Counting in Japanese

1	*Ichi*
2	*Ni*
3	*San*
4	*shi / (yon)*
5	*Go*
6	*Roku*
7	*Nana/(shichi)*
8	*Hachi*
9	*Kyū/(ku)*
10	*Jū*
11	*Jū-ichi*
12	*Jū-ni*
13	*Jū-san*
14	*Jū-shi/(yon)*
15	*Jū-go*

16	*Jū-roku*
17	*Jū-nana* / *(shichi)*
18	*Jū-hachi*
19	*Jū-kyū*
20	*Ni-jū*
30	*San-jū*
40	*Yon-jū* *(shi-jū)*
50	*Go-jū*
60	*Roku-jū*
70	*Nana-jū (shichi jū)*
80	*Hachi-jū*
90	*Kyū-jū*
100	*Hyaku*

Generally speaking, you do not have to remember beyond 10. If you can learn these first, you will be able to see how they are combined to make bigger numbers.

Greetings before and after training

We use the following terms frequently, so it is useful to know them if you study *kendo*.

Before training

Onegai shimasu

This phrase is used often in Japan to ask someone to do something .So what does this mean in *kendo*?

It means, "please train with me". We are asking our training partners to train with us, so we say this while bowing. We also say this before matches with a bow.

After Training

Arigatō gozaimashita

You should always say "Thank you" after training. "*Arigatō gozaimashita*" means "Thank you very much" and is politer than just saying "*arigatō*", which is the equivalent of "Thanks". You can listen to the pronunciation here.[13]

<u>General terms in *kendō*</u>

Some of the words heard in *kendō* are foreign even to ordinary Japanese people.

Rei : Bow. So when someone says "*REI*", that means you bow.

Shōmen/Shinzen : *Shōmen* is the front of a *dojo*. *Shinzen* refers to the altar that traditional *dojo* have in the centre. *Shōmen* is more common now.

Sensei : Means "teacher". School teachers are also called *sensei* as well, as are dance teachers etc.

Hai : This means "yes" in Japanese. After *sensei* or someone tells you what to do, or teaches something, we have to respond with "*Hai*!".

Shinai : Bamboo sword

Bokutō / Bokken : Wooden sword

Keiko-gi : We usually call the top a *keiko-gi*, which means "training top". It is also called *kendōgi*.

Hakama : The split-skirt we wear in *kendō*. It looks like a skirt, but it is actually a pair of incredibly flared pants.

Kiai : It often refers to the "shout" or "scream". However, it also means internal energy. For beginners, the scream is considered to be a gauge of your energy level; so the louder your *kiai* is, the more energetic you are.

Hajime : This means "to start" or "to begin".

Yame : This means "Stop".

Seiza : This is how we sit (kneel) in *kendō*.

Mokusō : This is usually translated as "meditation". However, do not try to "meditate" if you are a beginner. Simply breathe in and out quietly. Feel and enjoy the silence.

Sage-tō : When you hear this command, just relax your arms. When you walk around with your sword, you are always in the *sage-tō* position i.e. simply carrying your sword in your left hand.

Tai-tō : *Tai* means "to wear" and "*tō*" means "sword", so this means "Wear your sword" i.e. hold it by your left side as if it was inserted in your belt.

Nuke-tō : *Nuke* means "to draw" and "*tō*" means "sword", so this means "draw your sword".

Sonkyo : Squat as if you are resting on your heels (refer to the picture on p.39). This is another way of showing respect.

Kamaete : This means "to assume a [fighting] stance". When you hear this command, you usually take *chūdan* (the basic middle stance).

---

[13] http://www.kendo-guide.com/terminology_onegai_shimasu.html

Osame-tō : "*Osame*" is to "put back", and "*tō*" means "sword", so this means put your sword back into your scabbard or *saya*. Usually when we hear "*Osame*", we sit in *sonkyo*, and with the "*tō*", we put our swords back into our *saya* (i.e. to our left waist) so we are in the *tai-tō* position.

Kamae-tō ; It sounds similar to "*kamaete*" and people often confuse this with *osame-tō*. But when you hear this command, you usually take *chūdan* straight from the *sage-tō* position. However, do not forget to take *tai-tō* first. Do not just squat down in *sonkyo*.

Men : Head target. Also the name of the mask.

Kote : Forearm (wrist) target. Also the name of the protective gloves.

Dō : Torso target. Also the name of the body protector.

Tsuki : Throat target.

Tare : Lower-body protector.

Himo : String, strap, cord.

These terms are probably enough to know at the early stage of your *kendō* career, but will be used all of the time in the *dōjō*. It may be confusing at first, but you will come to remember the words eventually.

7. KENDŌ BASICS BY KENDŌ GUIDE FOR BEGINNERS

We all have to go through the basics. No one starts *kendō* in armour. Even after putting armour on, we still work on the basics (in more advanced ways). Learning the basics is a never-ending process.

What are included in basics training?

- How to bow in the standing and sitting position
- *Shizentai* : *Shizentai* is the natural standing posture we learn at the beginning
- *Tai-tō*
- *Chūdan*: how to assume *chūdan*, and how to put your sword back
- Footwork : *suri-ashi, okuri-ashi, hiraki-ashi, ayumi-ashi, tsugi-ashi*
- *Suburi* : *jōge-buri, naname (sayū) jōge-buri*
- *Men-uchi* : *san-kyodō, ni-kyodō, ikkyodo*
- *Kote-uchi* : *san-kyodō, ni-kyodō, ikkyodō*
- *Dō-uchi* : *san-kyodō, ni-kyodō, ikkyodō* (only the right *dō*)
- *Nidan-uchi* : *Zenshin-kōtai Shōmen-uchi, Niho-zenshin Niho-kōtai Shōmen-uchi, Kote -and-Men, Kote -and-Dō*
- *Sayū-men-uchi*
- *Fumikomi* : Learning the stamping footwork
- *Chōyaku-shōmen-uchi (Haya-suburi)*

COLUMN: KENDŌ AND AGE

Many people worry about their age when starting *kendō*. Believe it or not, *kendō* can be practiced as long as you can move. Older practitioners can still spar with younger challengers who cannot even hit them. Of course, you do need some physical strength and endurance for *kendō*, but you will get stronger as you train. The article, 'How to increase my stamina for kendo?[14]' offers some helpful hints.

You may not be able to move as fluidly as people who have trained in *kendō* since they were children, but it is not useful to compare yourself with them. There are different levels in *kendō*. Ten year old children do ten year old *kendō*. 50 year old people have their own style. Age might seem like a disadvantage, but older people have more life experience, and you can do *kendō* in a different way than younger people. My father started kendo when he was 55. He made it to 5-*dan*. Sadly, he died of cancer the year he was aiming for 6-*dan*. It was not easy for him to train with other kendoists who had done kendo their entire lives, but he improved little by little. His story can be read here.[15]

We never throw punches and kicks to our opponents, and we do not have any throws, so *kendō* is really one of the safest martial arts to take up. Even though we are well-protected by armour, sometimes people accidentally hit you off target. It hurts a little, but it is never serious.

Even though *kendō* is the safest martial art, we do train ourselves by physically pushing ourselves to the limit. So if you are in your 30s or 40s, even 50s, you have to challenge your physical limitations. Your teacher may give you a hard training once in a while for this purpose. Don't take it personally. See it as an opportunity to improve yourself. Nevertheless, it is very important for you to talk to your *sensei* if you have physical difficulties. You should train hard, but not to the extent that you get hurt. Take it easy and try to acquire the *kendō* movements slowly but correctly. If you learn them correctly, you can improve a lot faster than you think, regardless of age.

---

[14] http://www.kendo-guide.com/how-to-increase-my-stamina-for-kendo.html

[15] http://www.kendo-guide.com/unknown_kendoist.html

8. HOW TO SIT IN SEIZA IN KENDŌ

There are many people who sit in *seiza* incorrectly even though *seiza* is an important part of *kendō* and Japanese culture.

Summary
* *Taitō* first
* Left foot first
* Quietly put your *shinai* down
* Place your *shinai* with the *tsuba* next to your left knee

When you sit in *seiza*, kneel down from the left foot, and stand up from the right. Why? If you think of how you draw your sword, it is easy to see why. When you draw your sword, your right foot moves forwards. You must not look down when you sit. Keep your body balanced, and do not let it sway as you go up and down. Put your *shinai* down without making a noise. In other words, treat it with respect. It will make a noise if you put your hands down before your knees. Check the videos on how to sit in *seiza* with a sword.[16] Please watch them so you know how to sit in *seiza* properly. The pictures below show how to sit in *seiza* without a sword.

1. Slide the left foot backwards

2. The left knee on the floor

3. Both knees on the floor

4. Complete the *seiza* position

---

[16] http://www.kendo-guide.com/how_to_sit_in_seiza.html

COLUMN: NEW IN BŌGU AND STRIKES ARE PAINFUL?

When you put a set of *bōgu* on for the first time you will undoubtedly be quite excited. This is the time when people smile the most, but they soon realise that wearing *bōgu* comes with being hit, and this can be quite a shock for some. It seems that many people never thought about the idea of getting hit. Beginners are so used to striking advanced students that they never expect to get struck back.

Bōgu is designed to protect us, but you will feel tinges of pain or reverberations. I am not trying to scare you, but prepare you. Remember that's the discomfort others are feeling when you strike them, but is how we improve our striking technique. In any case, there will always be an element of discomfort at first, and you may get struck (or strike) unprotected areas by accident, so please do not forget to bow with appreciation and respect before and after you train with a person. This is very important.

However, if you come up against a caveman whose strikes are so painful that you think a bone might be broken if you continue, then you can be forgiven for bowing out. Some people strike too powerfully (like an axe), and if you are not used to receiving, it can be very painful to have to deal with. Also, make sure that your *bōgu* fits you properly. If it is too loose or too tight, it will not stop the hurt!

If you start feeling pain during training (psychologically or physically) avoid lowering your head or lifting your shoulders up when receiving *men* strikes. If you do this, it will hurt even more, so try to stand up straight and keep the back of your neck erect to prevent getting hit on top of the head.

Tsutsu, or the wrist part up of the *kote* (not the fist) should not be too tight. Some people try to tighten the strings like they are putting on boxing gloves, but if it is too constricted you will receive the impact of the *kote* strike directly on your arm. If you feel too much pain in your right arm when receiving *kote* strikes, you can buy a special protector to put on your wrist under the *kote*. As I said, if you feel pain when getting struck, instead of blaming the strikers you may want to talk to your teacher or more advanced students to improve your receiving skills.

9. HOW TO BOW IN THE STANDING AND SITTING POSITIONS

Japanese people bow a lot. When you greet someone in Japan, you generally bow to them. When you say goodbye, you also do so through bowing. You bow when you apologise, and you bow when you show appreciation. In *kendō* or any Japanese martial art, bowing is to show your respect to your opponent. An often quoted phrase is "*Rei ni Hajimari, Rei ni Owaru*". It means, "Start with bow, and end with bow". The word "*Rei*" also means "respect". So the phrase really means,

"Start with a bow to show respect to your opponent, and then finish the engagement with a bow to show your respect and gratitude to your opponent."

Two Bows

There are two kinds of bows. One is a standing bow (*ritsurei*), and the other one is the seated bow (*zarei*).

Ritsurei: There are two standing bows. One is to your opponent, and the other one even more formal to the *shōmen*. The difference between them is the angle of the bow.

   1. When bowing to your opponent, keep your body in the *shizentai* position. Bend your upper body from the hips while looking at your opponent. The angle of the bow is about 15 degrees, and you should always maintain eye-contact.

   * Point: Keep your chin in.

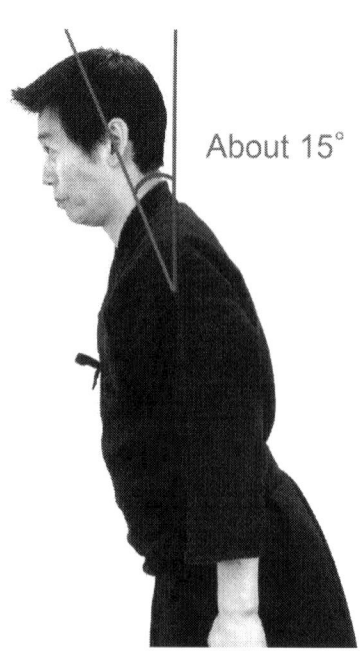

2: When bowing to teachers, higher ranks, and the *shōmen* (the front), lower your gaze. The angle of the bow is 30 degrees.

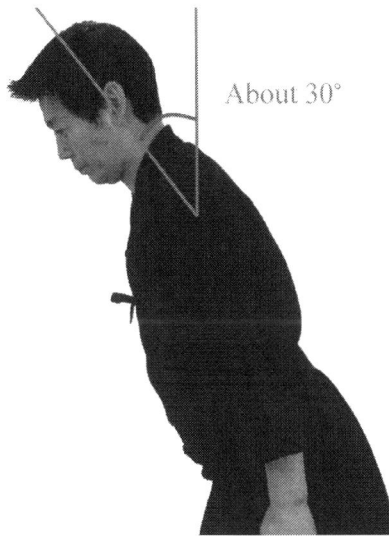

Zarei: From *seiza*, slowly and quietly lower your head down as you slide your hands from the top of your thighs down to the floor. Pause a while, then slowly lift your head up and return to the upright position.

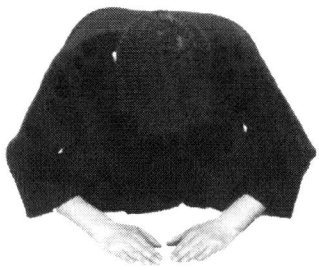

Make a triangle with the index fingers and thumbs of both hands. Lower your head as if your nose goes into the triangle. Look at the above picture carefully.

When you lower your head, keep your eyes open so that you can still maintain visibility.

*Points: When you lower your head, do not lift up at the hips or roll your shoulders. Also, avoid sticking your elbows out. Keep your neck and back straight. The big toe of the right foot should be on top of the left toe. You may find these videos helpful. [17]

---

[17] http://www.kendo-guide.com/how_to_sit_in_seiza.html

10. MOKUSŌ BREATHING: QUIET BUT POWERFUL
General Information on Breathing in *Kendō*

The correct method for breathing in *kendō* is not so complicated, and there are several ways of respiration such as that used in *zen*, yoga and so on.

Benefits of Breathing Properly

There is more than one method of breathing. Why is breathing methodology emphasized so much? What are the benefits of "proper" breathing?

- Improves our immunity so we do not get sick as often
- Makes us feel more energetic
- Helps our brain to function well
- Helps us to concentrate (intensity and duration)
- Increases our physical endurance
- Help us not to get tired or fatigued easily
- Helps us to remain calm
- Helps us to control our emotions

The basic procedure for respiration in *mokusō* is as follows:

1. Breathe in for 3 seconds
2. Hold your breath for 2 seconds
3. Breathe out for 10-15 seconds.

How do we do this?

1. Breathe in

Breathe in through your nose and take your breath down to a place called the *seika-tanden* (about three fingers under the navel). Avoid breathing lightly. Our shoulders often rise when we inhale, and it may seem that we are taking in a lot of air when we are not. If we breathe into our stomach or abdomen instead of our chest, we can take in a lot more air. Chest breathing is not good for *kendō* as we want to avoid showing opponents when we inhale as it is a tell-tale sign for a striking opportunity.

2. Hold your breath

Do not exhale immediately after breathing in. Hold your breath in the *seika-tanden* for about 2 seconds.

3. Breathe out

Breathe out through our mouth, but not at once. Exhale for about 10 - 15 seconds. Why so long? Because the longer it takes to exhale, the more control we have. In order to do so we have to use our abdominal muscles.

Here are some important points:

- Do not breathe out completely. Leave a bit of the air inside so you do not start gasping for air. Try to breathe out for 10 seconds, and gradually make your exhalations longer.

- Do not think about "emptying your mind" too much when sitting in *mokusō*. People TRY not to think about superfluous things, which means, paradoxically, that they already are. Just relax, and concentrate on the breathing. You can think about what you are going to improve on in training and so forth. Just relax and enjoy the *mokusō* moment.

This is basic breathing. Some people may suggest a different durations for each action (inhale, hold, exhale), but what I have introduced here is the standard. *Mokusō* breathing method may be difficult to learn, but as we do this at the beginning and end of training, thinking about doing it properly each time will lead to rapid improvement.

11. SHIZENTAI

Shizentai means "natural posture", but in actuality it may not be your **ordinary posture**. You must learn the natural posture in order to stand "naturally", and this directly relates to the quality of your *kamae*.

The key points are:

- Straighten the back of your neck
- Pull your chin in
- Tighten your buttocks

It does not sound like a natural posture, and it may feel uncomfortable the first time you try. There is a difference between being **relaxed** and being **lazy**. We need to make an effort to keep our posture straight but relaxed at the same time.

Upper Body:

1. Lift your shoulders
2. Bring your shoulders back (it feels like your shoulder blades are meeting at the back)
3. Drop your shoulders

1. Shoulders up

2. Shoulders back

Your chest will puff out naturally preventing your shoulders from rolling forwards.

4. Keep your chin in, but not too much
5. Keep the back of your neck straight

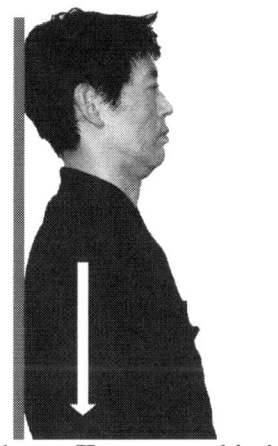

3. Shoulders down. Keep your chin in.

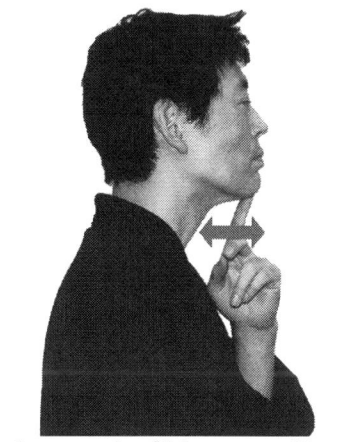

Bad example: Chin protruding

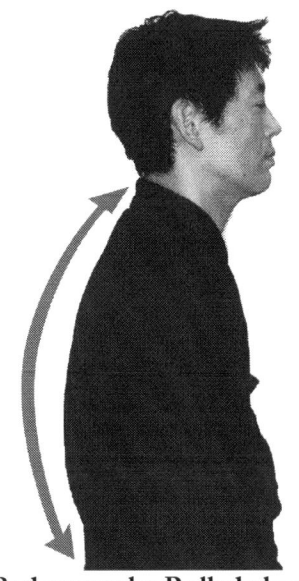

Bad example: Rolled shoulders

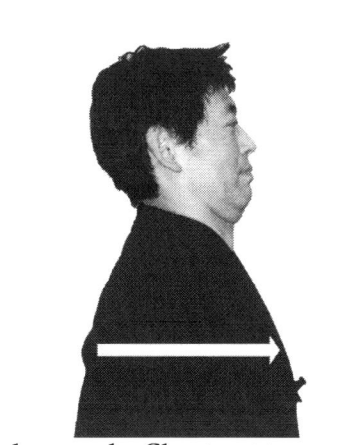

Bad example: Chest out too much

Lower Body:

1. Tighten your buttocks
2. Heels together, and toes apart (45 degrees between toes)

When you tighten your buttocks, you probably will feel your abs and hamstrings tighten too. You should feel taller. Do it until it becomes "natural". Please refer to the *shizentai* video.[18]

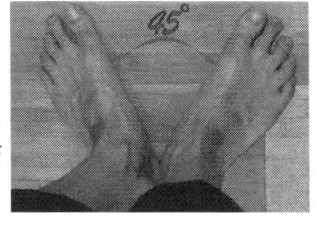

---

[18] http://www.kendo-guide.com/shizentai.html

12. TAITŌ

Taitō (*tai-tō*) is a command which means "wear your sword" at the hip. *Sagetō* is the position where sword is held in the left hand when walking or waiting. See Picture 1.

The *tsuka-gashira* (butt end of the grip) must be kept within your bodyline.

Sagetō position

When you hear the command "*Taitō!*", lift your left hand to your waist. This is actually representative of a *samurai* inserting his sword through his sash at the hip.

Taitō **position**

The *tsuka-gashira* should be in the centre of your body.

Tsuka-gashira **in the centre of the body**

Some *kenjutsu* schools preferred to place the *tsuba* (hand guard) in the centre of the body, but in modern *kendō* we keep the *tsuka-gashira* in line with the centre of the body.

<<NOTE>>

Point 1: When you wear a sword it should not come up higher than your waist. Some people tend to lift the rear end of the sword higher than the *tsuka-gashira* through gripping it too tight.

Point 2: Some bow in and out with their *shinai* in the *taitō* position, but this is incorrect. Bow in and out in the *sagetō* position.

Point 3: "Lock" your sword with the left thumb as shown below.

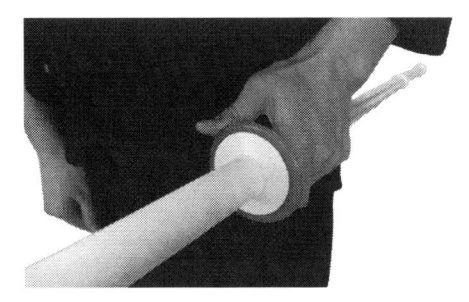

Point 4: The thumb should be placed off the centre of the *shinai* because, in theory, you would cut your thumb with the blade if it was a real sword.

Point 5: The right hand should be touching the right thigh. Please refer to the *taitō* video.[19]

---

[19] http://www.kendo-guide.com/taito.html

13. CHŪDAN

Chūdan is the most basic stance in *kendo*, so it is imperative that we learn it properly. There are two ways to assume the *chūdan* position:

1. *Chūdan* directly from *sagetō*
2. *Chūdan* after squatting in *sonkyo*

Chūdan from *sonkyo* is done in the following way:

1. Take *taitō*
2. On the command, "*Nuketō*", draw your sword
3. Squat down into *sonkyo*
4. Rise up into the *chūdan* position

How should you draw your sword?

<u>*Nuketō*</u>

On this command, push your *shinai* slightly forwards (**Picture 1**). Take a small step forwards onto the right foot and start drawing your *shinai* towards your opponent.

* When drawing the *shinai* with the right hand, the left hand stays motionless.

Flip your sword forwards as if you were attempting to slash your opponent, then take hold of the *shinai* with the left hand also. You should be ready to go. That means you are in the *chūdan* position. You can watch the movements in 'how to take *chūdan*' video.[20]

Picture 1: Front   **Picture 1: Side**

---

[20] http://www.kendo-guide.com/take_chudan.html

<u>*Osametō*: How to put your sword back into the *saya*</u>

Osame means "to put something back to where it came from", *osametō* is to put our sword back to the *saya* (scabbard). When you hear "*Osame-tō*", return your *shinai* back to the *taitō* position.

1. Squat in *sonkyo*

2. Return your sword back to the *taitō* position

3. Stand up and

4. Quietly lower the left hand

(the *sagetō* position)

When you return your sword to the *taitō* position while squatting in the *sonkyo* position, place your right hand on your upper thigh. Relax your right elbow and close the right arm pit. This prevents your right elbow from protruding too much. *Osametō* is an important movement in *kendō*, so please learn it well.

When returning the *shinai* or *bokutō* back to the *saya*, lift the *shinai* up into the *taitō* position.

<u>Putting your sword away without sitting in *sonkyo*</u>

When you hear the command, "*Sagetō!*", return your sword to the *sagetō* position without sitting in *sonkyo*. The sequence is as follows:

1. Return to the *taitō* position from *chūdan*

2. Lower the sword into the *sagetō* position

The most difficult part is understanding the commands. This will come with time, but try to become familiar with them as soon as possible.

14. HOW TO GRIP THE SHINAI PROPERLY

It goes without saying that it is very important to know how to grip your sword correctly. Yet I see many people cannot do it properly. Here, I will introduce **three ways** that are effective for beginners to learn how to grip a *shinai*. First, the most common problem with griping a *shinai* is the "punching fist".

Bad Grip

This is **NOT** a good grip in *kendo* because it decreases flexibility in the wrists. This means that you will not be able to strike crisply with *sae* (sharpness), especially with small cuts. Refer to "How do I know if I'm striking too hard?"[21] and "How to have good *tenouchi*".[22] A good grip in *kendo* is essential.

Good Grip

I believe that in order to have a good grip in *kendo*, we need to know what a good grip looks like. We can all make this grip when we don't have a *shinai* in our hands, so what's the problem?

How to keep that shape when we have a *shinai* in our hands.

---

[21] http://www.kendo-guide.com/how-do-i-know-if-im-striking-too-hard.html

[22] http://www.kendo-guide.com/terminology_tenouchi.html

An umbrella holds the key. In my video "How to Learn *Kendo* Movements More Easily and Quickly"[23], I introduce the "ice cream cone grip". The problem is that you can't have an ice cream in the *dojo*! So enter the umbrella. An umbrella is an ideal tool because of its shape. Make sure that the little finger grips the thinner end of the umbrella.

Because of its conical shape, you will be able to get the feeling of what a good grip is. You can easily tighten the left little and ring fingers. These fingers must be tense at all times. Because of the round shape of the *shinai* handle (*tsuka*), it is difficult for beginners to understand the right feeling in the hands. Still not working? What about when you hold it up in the rain? Does it resemble the *kendo* grip? Most of the time it does.

It is hard to grab an umbrella like the picture below and have our elbow relaxed (without sticking out to the side).

---

[23] http://www.kendo-guide.com/How-to-Learn-Kendo-Movements-More-Easily-and-Quickly.html

If this is not working for you how about…

The Pen Grip

I realised that the way I hold a pen is similar to gripping a *shinai*.

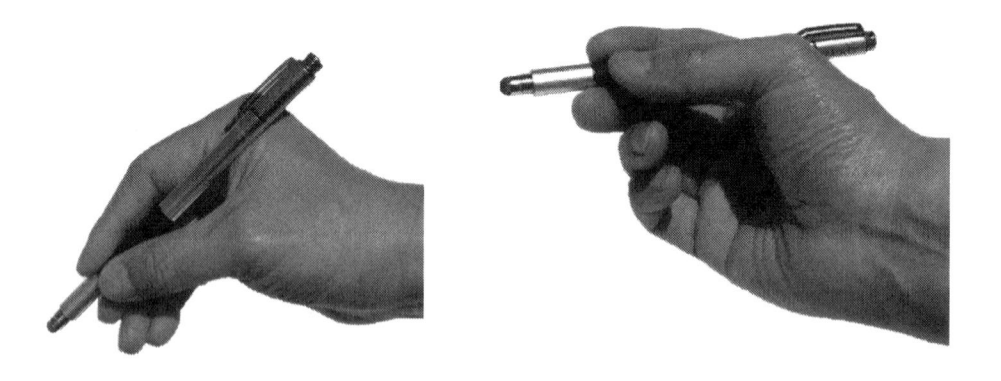

This is how I grip a pen. Now if I change the position of that pen like I grab a *shinai*…

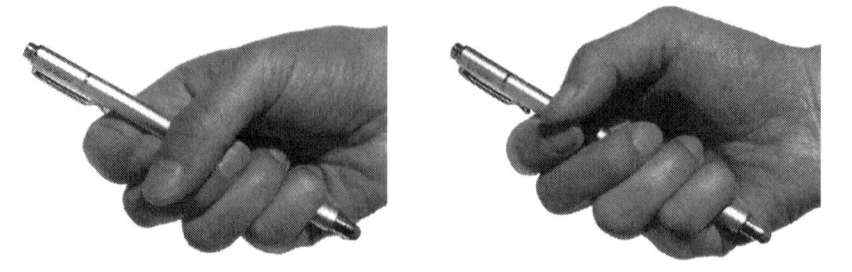

This will only work if you grip your pen like me. So I was thinking…

Ichiban!

If you make this No.1 sign, you will have the right shape for *kendō* grip with the exception of the index finger.

Then all you have to do is to roll your index back in.

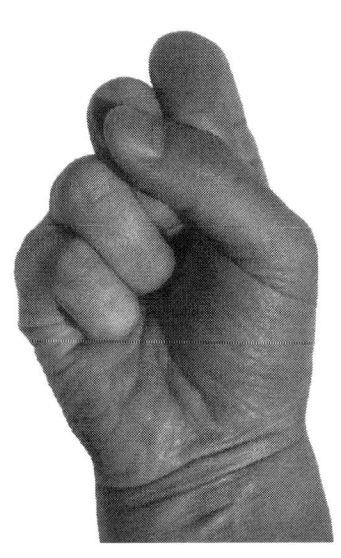

I think this is fairly effective, so the next time you pick up your *shinai*, try one of the methods introduced here if you are having trouble the grip. Now you know what the correct grip looks, so maybe you can come up with your own method for remembering.

COLUMN: HOW CAN YOU TELL IF AN INSTRUCTOR IS GOOD OR NOT?

I have dealt with this question on the Q&A section of my website and it was a hard question to answer. Usually, in Japan if someone starts bragging about their *kendo*, they are not deemed to be very good teachers. They may be able to teach you techniques, but not the *kendō* mind. However, through living in New Zealand and Guatemala, I learned how important self-promotion as an instructor is. To prospective students, it seems that it is important for to know what the instructor has achieved in the past in deciding whether or not to study under him or her. This is the reason why I introduce my *sensei*, and what I have achieved personally in the past in my profile.[24] Even so, I do feel slightly awkward in doing this.

Here are some tips for knowing how to choose a good teacher. It is usually a bad sign when people start talking up their own skills while talking others down. This is not a true attitude of a kendoist as even teachers are still students of the Way. One of my teachers, Miyazaki *sensei*, is always trying to improve his *kendō* so every time I train with him, something is different. He is very strong but incredibly humble at the same time.

There is an old saying, "You should spend three years searching for a good teacher rather than starting three years earlier." To start learning early is fine, but learning from a good teacher is a lot better. If you are lucky to have a *dōjō* near where you live, you should go and observe the teachers and students first. Listen to what the teachers tell their students, and what the students are talking about. Pay particular notice to etiquette and manners, and how everybody acts in the *dōjō*, how they treat their *shinai*, how they bow to each other, etc.

Sensei is a common word for teacher. Everyone can be a *sensei*, but not everyone can be a *shishō* or *shi* — or "master". *Shi* can teach *kendo*, and also about life in general. You may be able to find a teacher, but you really want a good *shishō* who you can follow for the rest of your life.

---

[24] http://www.kendo-guide.com/profile.html

15. BASIC KENDŌ FOOTWORK

Footwork is *ashi-sabaki* in Japanese. There are 5 *ashi-sabaki* in *kendō*.

- *Suri-ashi*
- *Okuri-ashi*
- *Tsugi-ashi*
- *Ayumi-ashi*
- *Hiraki-ashi*

Suri-ashi

Suri-ashi is the way we perform a considerable amount of *kendō* footwork. It is basically a sliding movement which we learn first. In the basic stance, *chūdan*, our right foot is in front, and the left foot is back with the left heel slightly raised. However when we move it is much easier if we lift both heels up slightly. What does "slightly" mean? Just enough to put a piece of paper between your heel and the floor. The left heel is higher than the right heel in preparation to lunge forward.

Okuri-Ashi

This is the most important method footwork, and is also the most difficult. You must learn it well…

Basic Stance

In the basics, the right foot is in front, and the left foot is back with the left heel slightly up.

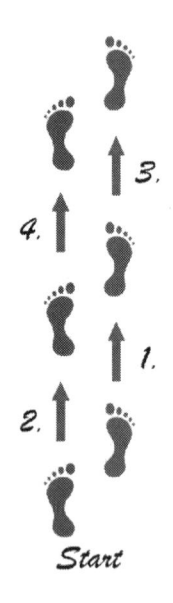

When moving forwards, move from the front foot first.

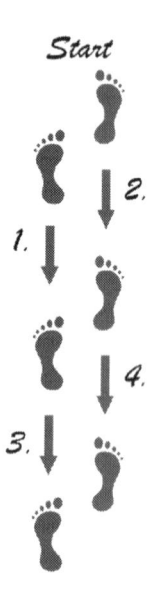

When moving backwards, move from the back foot first. In *okuri-ashi*, the back foot **never** passes the front foot regardless.

Some Important Points

* It is very common for beginners to **drag** their feet, especially the back foot when they perform this *ashi-sabaki*. Never do this.

Zenshin Kōtai Okuri-Ashi

This is *okuri-ashi* going forwards and backwards. *Zenshin* means advance and *kōtai* is retreat..

COMMAND

1. ***Zenshin Kōtai Okuri-ashi, Hajime!** (**Hajime** means start or begin)*
2. ***Mae***
3. ***Ato***
4. ***Yame*!**

Continue repeating steps 2 and 3 until the instructor shouts "*Yame* (Stop)". When practitioners get used to *ashi-sabaki*, the instructor does not have to say *Mae* and *Ato*. Practitioners keep moving and shouting until the instructor shouts *Yame*. In this exercise, take a step forward with the command of *Mae* and step backwards with the command of *Ato*.

KIAI

Practitioners shout "EI!" when advancing and "YEAH!" when retreating. Practice this without a *shinai* first to get used to the movement.

Niho Zenshin Niho Kōtai Okuri-Ashi

Niho means two steps. In this exercise, with the command "*Niho Zenshin Niho Kōtai Okuri-Ashi*", take two steps forwards and two backwards.

COMMAND

1. ***Niho Zenshin Niho Kōtai Okuri-Ashi, Hajime!***
2. ***Mae, Mae***
3. ***Ato, Ato***
4. ***Yame*!**

Continue repeating steps 2 and 3 until the instructor shouts *Yame*.

When the practitioners are used to the *ashi-sabaki*, the instructor does not have to say *Mae* and *Ato*. Practitioners keep moving and shouting until the instructor shouts *Yame*. In this exercise, take two steps forwards on the command of "*Mae, Mae*", and two steps back with the command "*Ato, Ato*".

KIAI

Practitioners shout "EI!, EI!" with each step forward, and "YEAH!, YEAH!" with each step back.

Shihō Ashi-Sabaki

Shihō means "four directions". On this command, take a step forward, backward, to the right and to the left respectively.

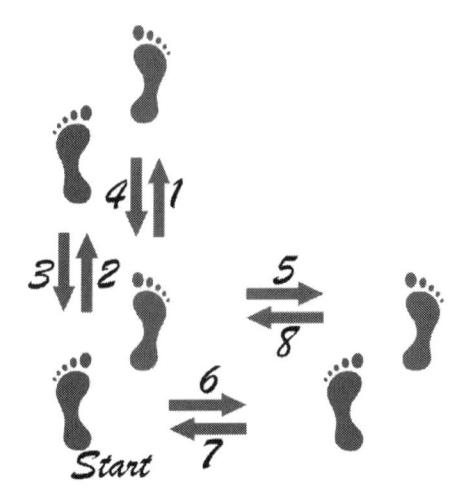

Before learning this, you should briefly practice *okuri-ashi* to the right and left. You do not have to take much time with this *ashi-sabaki* before moving onto *shihō ashi-sabaki*.

COMMAND

1. ***Shihō Ashi-Sabaki, Hajime!***
2. ***Mae***
3. ***Ato***
4. ***Migi*** (right)
5. ***Hidari*** (left)
6. ***Yame!***

Continue repeating steps 2 through 5 until the instructor shouts *Yame*. When the practitioners are used to the *ashi-sabaki*, the instructor does not have to say *Mae*, *Ato*, *Migi* and *Hidari*. Practitioners keep moving and shouting until told to stop.

KIAI

The practitioners shout "EI!" when taking a step forwards and to the right, and "YEAH!" stepping backwards and to the left.

Hiraki-Ashi

This is advanced footwork. Unlike *tsugi-ashi* and *ayumi-ashi*, it is included in a basic *suburi* (empty cut) and is introduced at a fairly early stage.

This *ashi-sabaki* is used to change the body direction by pivoting on one foot. It should be acquired slowly but accurately with improvement in other *kendō* skills. From the basic stance, step diagonally onto the right foot followed by the left.

Movement 1

Move diagonally onto the left foot, followed by the right. The right foot becomes the back foot.

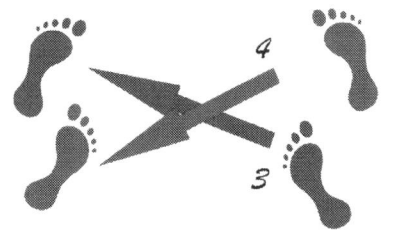

Movement 2

Go to the right as shown below.

Movement 3

Repeat from 2 to 3 until told to stop.

This footwork will be combined with *suburi* later. The remaining footwork are not taught to new beginners, but I will introduce them here for future reference.

Tsugi-Ashi

This is advanced footwork which is usually not learned until reaching the rank of *shodan*. In basic *kendō* footwork (*okuri-ashi*), the front foot must move first, but in the case of *tsugi-ashi*, the back foot moves first, and stops before passing the front foot. If the back foot passes the front foot, it is called *ayumi-ashi*, which is described below.

Ayumi-Ashi

In *ayumi-ashi* the feet are actually crossed just like normal walking.

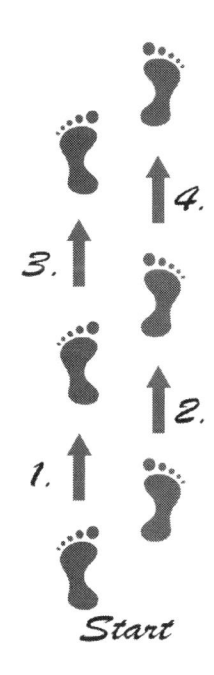

Refer to the following video showing *kendō* footwork.[25]

---

[25] http://www.kendo-guide.com/footwork.html

16. JŌGE-BURI

Jōge-buri (*jōge-buri*) is a type of empty cut (*suburi*) learned early on. *Jōge* means "up and down", and "*buri*" means "to swing". There are two types of *jōge-buri*:

- Basic *jōge-buri*
- *Naname* (*sayū*) *jōge-buri*

Basic *Jōge-Buri*

First of all, learn how to swing the sword without moving the feet. From *chūdan*, bring the hands right above your head. Simply bring your hands down and stop the sword when the tip reaches knee height.

<<SOME IMPORTANT POINTS>>

Do not allow the tip of the sword to touch your buttocks when you lift it overhead. If you do that, the little finger and the ring finger of the left hand naturally become loose. This will develop into a bad habit and it is very hard to fix. There is a way of doing this *suburi* like this, but I recommend that beginners not learn this method. It is more important to learn how to grip the sword firmly with the left pinkie and ring finger to start with.

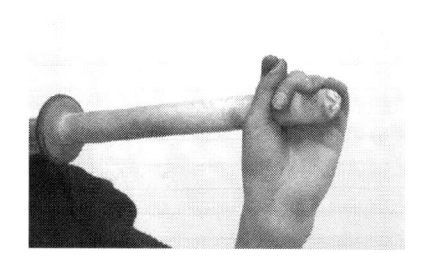

If the *kensaki* is too low,
the left palm will open

If the *kensaki* is at the right height,
the left palm won't open

When the tip of the sword is too low in the front, the left elbow will stick out. If you see yourself in the mirror, and notice that your left elbow is protruding, it is an indication that the tip of the sword is too low, and you will be able to see the inside of the left wrist. This is not desirable as it can also result in injury to your left wrists.

Bad example of *jōge-buri*

-- Don't Say *Men* –

When you practice *jōge-buri*, you should count instead of shouting *men*. The reason behind this is that we are not striking "*men*". *Jōge-buri* is to check your cuts such as *hasuji*, the angle of the blade. However, if your *dōjō*/club has you shout *men*, please do follow their custom.

Zenshin Kōtai Jōge-Buri

Once you have learned the *jōge-buri* movement, try to do it with *zenshin kōtai okuri-ashi*.

Going forwards

1. When stepping forwards onto the right foot, lift your sword up above your head.

2. When bringing the left foot forwards, bring the sword down to knee level.

1.   2.

Going backwards

1. Lift your sword above your head when stepping backwards onto the left foot.

2. When bringing the right foot back, your sword comes down to knee level.

1.

2.

Naname Jōge Buri

Naname means "diagonal", so in this form of *jōge-buri* the sword is swung up and down diagonally. This is called *sayū-jōge-buri* or *naname buri*. The basic process is exactly the same as *jōge-buri* but you swing your sword up and down diagonally, instead of vertically.

Strike *hidari*-m*en*

Cut through

Strike *migi-men*   Cut through

<<POINTS>>

-- Changing the direction of the sword --

Swing the sword up and down, and diagonally with clear angles. See the pictures above.

-- Your sword should be straight above your head --

When you bring your sword overhead, make sure that is straight like basic *joge-buri*. Bring the cut down on a diagonal.

-- Keep your left hand in the centre --

It is common for beginners to move both hands away from the centre of their body because they are concentrating on cutting diagonally. Your hands should not move from the centre of your body, especially your left hand.

-- Don't Say *Men* --

When you practice *jōge-buri*, you should count instead of shouting *men*. The reason behind this is that we are not striking "*men*". *Naname-jōge-buri* is to check your cuts such as *hasuji*, the angle of the blade. However, if your *dōjō*/club has you shout *men*, please do follow their custom.

Zenshin Kōtai Naname Jōge Buri

Once you acquired the *naname jōge-buri* movement, try it with *zenshin kōtai okuri-ashi*.

Going forwards

1. When stepping forwards from the right foot, bring your sword above your head.
2. When bringing the left foot up, your sword comes down to knee level.

Going backwards

1. When stepping back from the left foot, bring your sword above your head.
2. When bringing the right foot back, your sword comes down to knee level.

Here is a brief video of *jōge-buri*.[26]

---

[26] http://www.kendo-guide.com/jogeburi.html

COLUMN: IS IT TRUE THAT SOMEONE GOT BLINDED BY BROKEN SHINAI?

It is true. I was nearly stabbed in the arm with a broken *shinai*. As a matter of fact, once I found one inch splinter in my right forearm. *Kendō* is one of the safest *budō,* but tragedies can happen if we don't check our *shinai*. It is your responsibility to check and maintain your own *shinai* to protect your training partners. This cannot be emphasized enough. You do not need to check other peoples' *shinai*, just your own. Before training, you check your *shinai*. During training, you should check your *shinai*. You must constantly check your *shinai* for cracks or splinters.

If you see a splinter, don't assume it will be okay. Imagine if that splinter got in your eye. A splinter is a sign that the *shinai* is broken, and could inflict serious damage on your training partner when you strike them. Assume that your broken *shinai* could kill your partner. That's how serious it is. People who do not maintain their *shinai* should not be allowed to do *kendō*.

You should have more than two spare *shinai* on hand. I tell my students to have at least three that are in good condition. You never know how long a *shinai* will last. It may break as soon as you start to use it. That is why you should not buy *shinai* from just any martial arts shop. When it comes to *kendō* equipment, the key point is safety. Do not purchase the cheapest equipment you can find on the Internet.[27]

---

[27] http://www.kendo-guide.com/kendo-shop-review.html

17. MEN STRIKE: BASIC MEN TRAINING FOR BEGINNERS

The *men* strike (*men-uchi*) is probably the most important in *kendō*. Once you know how to strike *men*, it is an easier progression to *kote* (wrists) and *dō* (waist). Learn *men-uchi* step by step. There are 3 types:

1. ***San-kyodō (shō)men-uchi***
2. ***Ni-kyodō (shō)men-uchi***
3. ***Ikkyodō (shō)men-uchi***

Kyodō means "movement", so *san-kyodō* means three movements, *ni-kyodō* two movements, and *ikkyodō* one movement. The reason "*shō*" is in brackets is because some people say "*showmen*" instead of "*men*". It is good to know both.

San-kyodō (shō)men-uchi

First learn *san-kyodō*. There are three movements.

1. Lift your hands above your head from *chūdan*, and take a step forward from the right foot on the command "*Ichi!*".

2. Strike *men* on the command "*Ni!*"

3. Take a step back and return to *chūdan*.

COMMAND

1. *San-kyodo shomen-uchi, Hajime!*
2. *Ichi!*
3. *Ni!*
4. *San!*

Repeat 2 to 4 until told to stop.

KIAI

Practitioners shout, "*Men!*" while striking *men* on *Ni!*.

Some Important Points

It is often taught that the right hand should be at the height of the right shoulder when striking *men*. This is true when the practitioner is a child. For kids it is important to perform everything vigorously and without having to thinking too much. However, you will notice the tip of the sword (*kensaki*) is higher than your head if your right hand is at shoulder height.

That means you are not quite striking *men*. I suggest that adults keep their right hand lower than the right shoulder, and have the *kensaki* at eye-level when striking *men*.

The left hand will then be is as high as, or slightly lower than the solar plexus depending on how tall you are.

You do not have to spend too much time learning *san-kyodō*.

Ni-kyodō (shō)men-uchi

Two movements.

1. Lift your hands overhead from *chūdan*, and take a step forwards from the right foot to strike *men* with the command "*Ichi*!".
2. Take a step back and resume *chūdan* with "*Ni*".

COMMAND

1. *Ni-kyodō showmen-uchi, Hajime*!
2. *Ichi*!
3. *Ni*!

Repeat 2 to 3 until told to stop.

KIAI

Practitioners shout "*Men*!"

Ikkyodō (shō)men-uchi

Only one movement.

1. Lift your hands overhead from *chūdan* and take a step forwards from the right foot, strike *men*, take a step backwards and resume *chūdan*, all on the command "*Ichi*!".

COMMAND

1. *Ikkyodō shomen-uchi, Hajime!*
2. *Ichi!*

Repeat 2 until told to stop.

KIAI

Practitioners shout, "*Men*!"

These are methods for basic *men* strike training. Pease refer to this brief video for striking *men*.[28]

---

[28] http://www.kendo-guide.com/men_strike.html

COLUMN: KI KEN TAI ICCHI

気剣体一致

This is terminology that you absolutely need to know if you do *kendō*. (Some people say "*ki ken tai no itchi*".)

Ki: The Chinese word, *chi*, is more well-known than *ki* in the West, although the same *kanji* is used.

Ken: Sword, including *shinai*, *bokutō*, and *shinken*.

Tai: Body

Itchi: Synchronization

What does *ki-ken-tai-itchi* mean then? It means "to synchronize the movements of *ki*, *ken*, and *tai*". You cannot see *ki* so it usually refers to your shout or vocalization when striking. You have to declare where you are striking and synchronize your *ki* with your *shinai* and body. Only when you put everything together in the strike is it considered to be valid. It does not matter how many times you actually make contact with *men*, *kote*, *dō* or *tsuki*, you cannot score a point unless you have *ki-ken-tai-itchi*.

There is a similar sounding term that uses completely different *kanji*, and people quite often get confused by it — *ken-tai-itchi*. This word means "You should not just wait for your opponent to strike, and you should not attack randomly without analysing your opponent." This teaching is fairly advanced. *Ki-ken-tai-itchi*, on the other hand, must be practiced from the day you learn how to strike. Without knowing what it is and performing it, you will find it difficult to develop good *kendō*.

18. KOTE STRIKE: BASIC KOTE UCHI

Kote strike (*kote-uchi*) is relatively easy to do after learning the *men* strike. Change the height of your sword when you strike. *Kote* is lower than *men*.

Similar to *men* strike, learn *kote -uchi* step by step. There are 3 types;

1. ***San-kyodō kote-uchi***
2. ***Ni-kyodō kote-uchi***
3. ***Ikkyodō kote-uchi***

As explained in the *men* section, *kyodō* means "movement", so *san-kyodō* means three movements, and so on.

San Kyodō Kote Uchi

Learn *san-kyodo* first. There are three movements.

1. Lift your hands up high enough from *chūdan* so that you can see your opponent's *kote* and take a step forward from the right foot on the command, "*Ichi!*"

2. Strike *kote* on "*Ni!*"

3. Take a step back and resume *chūdan* on "*San!*"

COMMAND

1. *San-kyodō kote-uchi, Hajime!*
2. *Ichi!*
3. *Ni!*
4. *San!*

Repeat 2 to 4 until told to stop.

KIAI

Shout "*Kote!*"

<<Some Important Points>>

Don't lift your sword up as high as striking *men*. Also, not as much strength is needed in *kote* as it is for a *men* strike.

***Men* strike**   ***Kote* strike**

Men Strike   Kote Strike

Beginners tend to strike *kote* too hard to the extent that the receiver literally ends up with a swollen right wrist. Receivers (usually instructors or the more advanced practitioners) take many *kote* strikes per session. If there is even one person who strikes *kote* too powerfully, the receiver will be in agony for the rest of the training session. You should not strike *kote* with the same force as you strike *men*.

The height of the sword

It is parallel to the floor.

Many beginners do not know how low their sword should be when they strike a *kote*. It is important for instructors to emphasize to beginners the correct positioning of the sword at the conclusion of the strike.

Do not spend too much time on *San-kyodō kote-uch*. This is used to let practitioners know the process for striking, how far they should lift their hands, and the height of the *kote* strike.

Ni-kyodō kote-uchi

There are two movements.

1. Lift your hands up high enough from *chūdan* so that you can see your opponent's *kote*, and take a step forward from the right foot to strike *kote* on the command, "*Ichi*!".
2. Take a step back and resume *chūdan* on the command, "*Ni*!"

COMMAND

1. *Ni-kyodō kote-uchi, Hajime*!
2. *Ichi*!
3. *Ni*!

Repeat 2 and 3 until told to stop.

KIAI

The practitioner shouts "*Kote*!" while striking *kote* on the command of *Ichi*!

Ikkyodō Kote Uchi

We have only one movement.

1. Lift your hands from *chūdan* high enough so that you can see your opponent's *kote* and take a step forwards onto the right foot, strike *kote*, take a step backwards and go back to *chūdan* on the command, "*Ichi*".

COMMAND

1. *Ikkyodō kote-uchi, Hajime*!
2. *Ichi*!

Repeat 2 until the instructor shouts "*Yame*".

KIAI

The practitioners shout "*Kote*!" while striking on the command *Ichi*!

These are the methods for basic *kote* strike training. There is a brief video *kote* strikes at this URL.[29]

---

[29] http://www.kendo-guide.com/kote_strike.html

19. DŌ STRIKE: BASIC DŌ-UCHI

Dō strike (*dō-uchi*) is comparatively easy after learning *men* and *kote*. Lift your sword overhead as if striking strike *men*. However, we have to change the direction of the sword blade to cut our opponent's right torso, just under the ribcage.

Similar to *men*, there are 3 ways for practicing:

1. **San-kyodō dō-uchi**
2. **Ni-kyodō dō-uchi**
3. **Ikkyodō dō-uchi**

San-kyodō dō-uchi

First, learn how to do *san-kyodō*. There are three movements.

1. Lift your hands above your head from *chūdan* and take a step forwards from the right foot on the command "*Ichi!*".

2. Strike *dō* on "*Ni!*"

3. Take a step back and resume *chūdan* on "*San!*"

COMMAND

1. *San-kyodō dō-uchi, Hajime!*
2. *Ichi!*
3. *Ni!*
4. *San!*

Repeat 2 to 4 until the told to stop.

KIAI

**Bad Example
Lowering and moving
the sword away
from the centre**

Practitioners shout "*Dō!*" while striking on *Ni*!

Some Important Points

Overhead again

Bring your sword above your head as if striking *men*.

Turning your sword

It is easier for practitioners to understand what they should be doing if there is someone in front of them. In any case, the *dō* height is about the same as a *kote* height, but the angle of the sword is different. It should be angled diagonally down to the right. Change the direction of the sword using the wrists only. Some people tend to lean their body to the left to change the direction, but this is incorrect. Remember, always keep your body upright.

** Do not spend too much time on *san-kyodō dō-uchi***

Once the practitioners acquire how to change the direction of the sword, then you can move onto *Ni-kyodō dō-uchi*.

Ni-kyodō dō-uchi

There are two movements:

1. Lift your hands above your head from *chūdan* and take a step forward from the right foot and strike *dō* on "*Ichi*".

2. Take a step back and resume *chūdan* with "*Ni*."

COMMAND

1. *Ni-kyodo do-uchi, Hajime*!

2. *Ichi*!

3. *Ni*!

Repeat 2 to 3 until told to stop.

KIAI

The practitioners shout "*Dō!*" while striking on *Ichi*!

Ikkyodō Dō Uchi

There is only one movement.

1. Lift your hands overhead from *chūdan* and take a step forwards from the right foot, strike *dō* and take a step back and resume *chūdan* on *Ichi*!

   COMMAND

   1. *Ikkyodō dō-uchi, Hajime!*
   2. *Ichi!*

   Repeat 2 until told to stop.

   KIAI

Practitioners shout "*Dō!*" while striking on *Ichi*! These are the methods for basic *dō* strike training. Please refer to this brief video for *dō* strikes.[30]

---

[30] http://www.kendo-guide.com/do_strike.html

20. ZENSHIN-KŌTAI MEN STRIKE

Zenshin-kōtai men strike is a method of *suburi* (empty cut). Some people may call it *(shō)men-uchi*. The footwork used here is *okuri-ashi*. *Zenshin* means "going forwards", and *kōtai* means "going backwards". This is how *zenshin kōtai showmen-uchi* is executed.

Zenshin-kōtai showmen-uchi

1. While lifting your sword above your head, take a step forwards onto the right foot, just like we did in *kyodō men*.

2. As you strike men, snap the left foot forwards. Make sure that the left foot does not pass the right foot or get too close to the right foot.

3. Now we are going backwards. While lifting your sword up above your head, take a step backwards onto the left foot.

4. While striking *men*, snap the right foot backward.

Keep doing 1 to 4 until you hear "*Yame!*"

1. Sword up when stepping forward

2. Strike *men* as left foot comes forward

3. Sword up when stepping backwards

4. Strike *men* as right foot comes back

COMMAND

1. *Zenshin-kōtai shōmen-uchi. Hajime!*
2. *Ichi, Ni, San, Shi, Go, Roku, Shichi, Hachi, Kyū, Jū*
3. *Yame!*

Repeat the count from 1 to 10 as many times as you want. Then, command "*Yame!*"

KIAI

There are three ways.

1. Every time the instructor counts the practitioners shout "*Men!*"

Instructor: *Ichi*

Practitioners: *Men*

Instructor: *Ni*

Practitioners: *Men*

Instructor: *San*

Practitioners: *Men*

Instructor: *Jū*

Practitioners: *Men*

Instructor: *Ichi*

Practitioners: *Men*

and continue until

Instructor: *Yame!*

2. Or, everyone counts at the same time until they hear "*Yame!*" instead of shouting "*Men!*"
3. Or, everyone shouts *men* until they hear "*Yame!*"

I usually run my classes as explained for 1, but each *dōjō* is different.

<<Some Important Points>>

It is easy for beginners to strike *men* when going forwards, but it is difficult to coordinate the sword and footwork when stepping back. *Zenshin-kōtai shōmen-uchi* should be practiced carefully, paying attention to sword-footwork coordination. Not practicing this movement thoroughly will result in problems later when wearing armour.

Footwork

You should not lift the toes up in the footwork. Striking is the easy part, so concentrate more on doing the footwork correctly. Here is a brief video of *Zenshin-kōtai shōmen-uchi*.[31]

---

[31] http://www.kendo-guide.com/zenshin_kotai_men_strike.html

COLUMN: SHU HA RI
Training Phases

守破離

Shu-ha-ri is a teaching that outlines three phases in learning *kendō* or other traditional arts.

Shu usually means "to protect", but in this case it means to "maintain the teachings" or "to keep the promise." When you start learning something, you have to listen to your teacher and follow their instructions to the letter in order to acquire the basics correctly. Avoid the temptation to go somewhere else to get other information because you will become confused and cannot acquire the correct basics. That is why it is very important to CHOOSE the right teacher.

Ha means "to break". So, in the case of the arts, it means to dismantle the teachings you have acquired from your teacher and learn something new from others. It's not as disloyal as it sounds. Once you have learned the basics, you need to learn other things to improve yourself physically and mentally.

Ri means "to leave". In other words, you leave your teachers and establish your own style. It is the highest state of independence.

So how do we know which phase of *Shu-ha-ri* we are in? *Shu* is easy, as it is the very beginning. You are just like a newborn baby. You have to learn how to crawl, how to walk, how to grip and so on. You learn very basic skills during this phase. Maybe it takes five to ten years to develop solid basics. *Ha* is the next phase in which you meet new people. You will move in different circles with new teachers. On top of what you have learned from your previous teachers, you will discover new teachings and perspectives. This is also a stage in which you test the skills you have developed to date. It is a period of trial and error. This phase will last a long time. I have been studying *kendō* since 1980 and I am still in this phase. Going back to basics while learning new skills and philosophies is a daily routine. *Ri* is probably 7-*dan* and 8-*dan* level. You establish your own style based on what you have learnt, but that doesn't mean that you name your style something other than *kendō*. It simply means that you polish your skills and techniques in your own way, but always based on the established fundamentals.

21. NIHO-ZENSHIN NIHO-KŌTAI-MEN STRIKE

Niho-zenshin niho-kōtai-men is the next step after *zenshin-kōtai shōmen-uchi*. It seems easier to do because another step forwards and backwards is simply added, but always pay extra attention to each movement. The footwork used here is *okuri-ashi*. Footwork is more important in this training than striking. *Niho-zenshin* means "two steps forward", and *niho-kōtai* means "two steps back".

Niho-zenshin niho-kōtai shōmen-uchi

1. While lifting your sword up above your head, take a step forwards from the right foot.

2. As you strike *men*, snap the left foot in behind the right, making sure that it does not pass the right, or get too close.

3. Without going back into *chūdan* (i.e. from the *men* position), lift the sword overhead and take another step forwards from the right foot.

4. As you strike *men*, snap the left foot in behind the right, making sure that it does not pass the right, or get too close.

5. Now we go back. While lifting your sword overhead, take a step back from the left foot.

6. While striking *men*, snap the right foot back to a position in front of the left.

7. While lifting your sword overhead, take another step back from the left foot.

8. While striking *men*, snap the right foot back again.

Keep doing 1 to 8 until the instructor orders you to stop.

**1. Sword up
when stepping forward**

**2. Strike *men*
as left foot comes up**

**3. Sword up
when stepping forwards**

**4. Strike *men*
as left foot comes up**

**5. Sword up
when stepping back**

**6. Strike *men*
as right foot comes back**

**7. Sword up
when stepping back**

**8. Strike *men*
as right foot comes back**

COMMAND

1. *Niho-zenshin niho-kotai shomen-uchi. Hajime!*

2. *Ichi, Ni, San, Shi, Go, Roku, Shichi, Hachi, Kyū, Jū*
3. *Yame*!

Repeat the count from 1 to 10 and do several times.

KIAI

On each count, the practitioners strikes two *men* shouting "*Men, men*!"

Instructor: *Ichi*

Practitioners: *Men, men!* (going forwards)

Instructor: *Ni*

Practitioners: *Men, men* (going back)

Instructor: *San*

Practitioners: *Men, men* (going forwards)

.

Instructor: *Jū* (going back)

Practitioners: *Men, men*

Instructor: *Ichi* (going forwards)

Practitioners: *Men, men*

and continue until

Instructor: *Yame*!

Some Important Points

As I mentioned earlier, we need to concentrate on footwork more than striking in these exercises, otherwise it is harder to strike continuously. Striking will naturally faster and stronger through continuous practice so long as the footwork is correct. In the *zenshin-kōtai shōmen-uchi* section, I mentioned the importance of paying attention to sword-footwork coordination. We should have already acquired hand-foot coordination in *zenshin-kōtai shōmen-uchi* so *niho-zenshin niho-kōtai shōmen-uchi* should be easier to learn.

Footwork

The same as in *zenshin-kōtais shōmen-uchi*.

Don't lift your toes up.

The following is a brief video of *niho-zenshin niho-kōtai shōmen-uchi*[32].

---

[32] http://www.kendo-guide.com/niho-zenshin-niho-kotai.html

22. KOTE-MEN STRIKE: BASIC KOTE-MEN STRIKE IN SUBURI

This is the basic *kote-men* strike. *Kote-men* is a common technique in *kendō*, and is classified as *nidan-waza* (consecutive striking techniques). If your *sensei* tells you to do "*Kote oyobi men*" (*kote* and *men*), this usually means basic *kote-men* strike done in a large motion. *Kote-men* usually refers to a fast *kote* and *men* strike. Terminology depends on the *dōjō*. Once you have learned *niho-zenshin niho-kōtai*, this technique should be fairly easy to execute. All you have to do is to change the first strike from *men* to *kote*. The difficult part, however, is combining two different strikes correctly.

1. Bring your sword up to the appropriate height.
2. Ensure that your footwork is correct.
3. If you can do *niho-zenshin niho-kōtai shōmen-uchi* properly, this should be easy to learn.

Kote Oyobi Men-uchi

1. Lift your sword up until you can see the right *kote* of the opponent from under our left hand, and take a step forwards from the right foot. The step in should be smaller than when striking *men*.

2. Snap the left foot up while striking *kote*. Make sure that the left foot does not pass the right foot, or get too close.

3. Without going back into *chūdan* (i.e. from the *kote* position), lift the sword overhead and take another big step forwards from the right foot.

4. Snap the left foot up as you strike *men*. Make sure that the left foot does not pass the right foot or get too close.

5. While lifting your sword up until you can see the right *kote* of the opponent under left hand, take a step back from the left foot.

6. Snap the right foot backward while striking *kote*.

7. While lifting your sword overhead, take another step back from the left foot.

8. Snap the right foot back while striking *men*.

Keep doing 1 to 8 until told to stop.

1. Sword up
when stepping forwards

2. Strike *kote*
as left foot comes up

3. Sword up
when stepping forwards

4. Strike *men*
as left foot comes up

5. Sword up
when stepping back

6. Strike *kote*
as right foot comes back

**7. Sword up
when stepping back**

**8. Strike *men*
as right foot comes back**

COMMAND

1. *Kote oyobi men. Hajime!*

2. *Ichi, Ni, San, Shi, Go, Roku, Shichi, Hachi, Kyū, Jū*

3. *Yame!*

Repeat the count from 1 to 10 several times.

KIAI

On each count practitioners shout "*Kote, men!*"

Instructor: *Ichi*

Practitioners: *Kote , men!* (going forwards)

Instructor: *Ni*

Practitioners: *Kote , men* (going back)

Instructor: *San*

Practitioners: *Kote , men* (going forwards)

.

Instructor: *Jū* (going backwards)

Practitioners: *Kote , men*

Instructor: *Ichi* (going forwards)

Practitioners: *Kote*, *men*

and continue until

Instructor: *Yame*!

Some Important Points

Do not bring your hands completely above your head when striking *kote*. The overhead swing in a big *kote* strike is not as big as a *men* strike.

Footwork

Do not lift the toes up when moving and the left foot stays behind the right. Visit the page for "*kote oyobi men*"[33] and watch the video too.

---

[33] http://www.kendo-guide.com/basic_kote_men.html

23. KOTE DO STRIKE: BASIC KOTE DO STRIKE IN SUBURI

This is the basic *kote-dō* strike. You will notice how difficult *dō* strikes are when you put *bōgu* (armour) on. Eventually you will learn the faster version of *kote* and *dō* strikes, but do it slowly and accurately first. Once you have learned *kote oyobi men*, this techniques is relatively easy. All you have to do is to change the second strike from *men* to *dō*. Do not lift your sword overhead as high as in a *men* strike for *kote*, but the *dō* strike should be a big strike.

Kote oyobi dō-Uchi

1. Lifting your sword up until can see the right *kote* of our opponent, take a step forward from the right foot. The step should be smaller than when striking *men*.

2. As you strike *kote*, snap the left foot up. Make sure that the left foot does not pass the right foot, or get too close.

3. Without going back to *chūdan* (i.e. from the *kote* position), lift our sword overhead and take a big step forward from the right foot.

4. As you strike *dō*, snap the left foot up behind the right again. Make sure that the left foot does not pass the right foot or get too close.

5. While lifting your sword overhead far enough to see the right *kote* of your opponent under your left hand, take a step back from the left foot.

6. While striking *kote*, snap the right foot back in front of the left.

7. While lifting your sword overhead, take another step back from the left foot.

8. While striking *dō*, snap the right foot back.

Keep doing 1 to 8 until told to stop.

1. Sword up when stepping forwards

2. Strike *kote* as left foot comes up

**3. Sword up
when stepping forwards**

**4. Strike *dō*
as left foot comes up**

**5. Sword up
when stepping back**

**6. Strike *kote*
as right foot comes back**

**7. Sword up
when stepping back**

**8. Strike *dō*
as right foot comes back**

COMMAND

1. *Kote oyobi dō. Hajime*!
2. *Ichi, Ni, San, Shi, Go, Roku, Shichi, Hachi, Kyū, Jū*!
3. *Yame*!

Repeat the count from 1 to 10 several times.

KIAI

On each count, the practitioners shout "*Kote, dō!*"

Instructor: *Ichi*

Practitioners: *Kote, dō!* (going forwards)

Instructor: *Ni*

Practitioners: *Kote, dō* (going backwards)

Instructor: *San*

Practitioners: *Kote, dō* (going forwards)

..

Instructor: *Jū* (going backwards)

Practitioners: *Kote, dō*

Instructor: *Ichi* (going forwards)

Practitioners: *Kote, dō*

and continue until

Instructor: *Yame*!

Some Important Points

Do not bring your hands too far above your head when you strike *kote*.

Footwork

Do not lift the toes up when moving and the left foot stays behind the right. Visit the page of "*kote oyobi dō*"[34] and watch the video too.

---

[34] http://www.kendo-guide.com/basic_kote_do.html

24. SAYŪ-MEN: THE CORE MOVEMENT OF KIRIKAESHI

When learning *sayū-men*, it might be a little frustrating. It looks simple to do after learning *shōmen-uchi* but you will soon realise that it is hard to control the angle of the sword. There are some basic rules to follow. First, make sure that the blade angle is correct, and that it connects with the target at 45 degrees from the centreline.

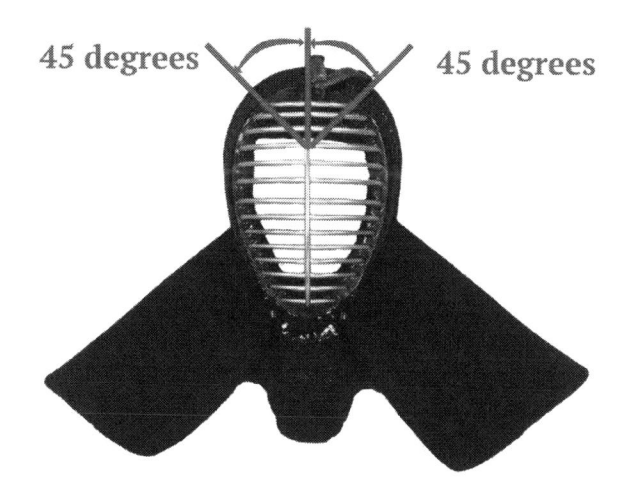

Second, keep your left hand in the centre. This is difficult if your left grip is too tight. "Too tight" means you are using all the left fingers to grab the sword, and every single finger is tense. Remember, you should use only the left ring finger and little finger to hold the sword tightly, and the rest of your fingers should be relaxed.

Bad grip
All fingers are tight.

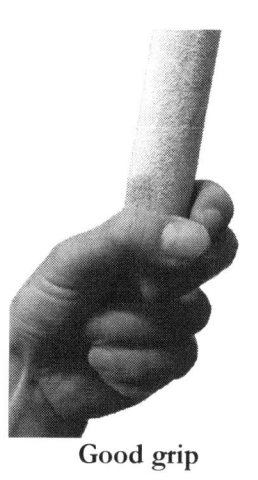

Good grip
Only the little finger and ring finger are tight.

This could be a big challenge for beginners. If you learn how to do *sayū-men* correctly, you will understand how the left hand should be used.

   **This video to shows how to grip your *shinai*.[35]

---

[35] http://www.kendo-guide.com/take_chudan.html

Third, since we say that the right hand is the control hand, people tend to try and change the angle of the sword using the right hand. Try and avoid using the whole right arm to change the angle of the sword. Just use the hands and wrists. You need to practice this over and over to acquire the correct movement, but remember not to use the whole arm to change the trajectory of the blade.

You should already know how to do *zenshin-kōtai shōmen-uchi* and *niho-zenshin niho-kōtai shōmen-uchi* by now. These are done in exactly the same way. The only difference is the angle of the sword. So, it is important to know how to change the angle of the sword correctly when practicing *sayū-men*. Here is a brief video of *sayū-men*.[36]

Striking the left *men* without *shinai*   **Striking the right *men* without *shinai***

---

[36] http://www.kendo-guide.com/sayumen.html

25. FIRST TIME FUMIKOMI? LEARN IT STEP BY STEP

I have already written two articles and made two videos dedicated to *fumikomi*. *Fumikomi* is one of the most difficult movements in *kendō*. If you have seen these articles and videos, please read this article as a review.

Why do we do fumikomi?

From *issoku-ittō-no-ma*[37], you have to reach your opponent with one step. Without *fumikomi*, covering the distance necessary will be quite difficult in one step. Even though *fumikomi* is translated as "lunge" or "stomping", the movement looks more like "jumping" forwards. To reach your training partner you should jump forwards, not up.

What makes fumikomi difficult?

The no.1 reason why people have difficulty is because they are trying to strike too hard. Many think that they cannot reach their training partner with one *fumikomi* so they try to make up the distance by stretching their arms out. This prevents them from learning the correct *fumikomi*.

How should we learn fumikomi?

Step by step. Always go back to basics such as *san-kyodo*. From there, try ease into *fumikomi*. You need to gradually get a feeling of what *fumikomi* is first. Then, incrementally make the distance further from your training partner as you gain in confidence.

How can we improve?

1. Be strong and keep trying

    We all know that it is hard, so don't give up. Try and keep trying. Nobody gets it right first go. It took me around 2 years to perform *fumikomi* properly.

2. Don't cheat

    Since it is hard to reach your opponent with one *fumikomi*, people tend to cheat and try to get closer before striking using *tsugi-ashi* or *ayumi-ashi*.[38] If you develop these bad habits, it makes it even harder to learn correct *fumikomi* for striking from *issoku-ittō-no-ma*.

Use your body rather than your brain

Once you know the mechanism, "just do it". It helps to imitate those who can perform *fumikomi* well. If there is no one around to imitate, try imitating mine. If you can't do it straight away, don't get disillusioned. Please refer to these videos:

Fumikomi mechanism[39]

How to practice *Fumikomi*[40]

Brief video of *Fumikomi*[41]

---

[37] http://www.kendo-guide.com/terminology_Issoku_Itto_No_Ma.html

[38] http://www.kendo-guide.com/footwork.html

[39] http://www.kendo-guide.com/fumikomi_mechanism.html

[40] http://www.kendo-guide.com/practice_fumikomi.html

[41] http://www.kendo-guide.com/first_time_fumikomi.html

26. HAYA-SUBURI: JUST THE SAME AS OTHER SUBURI

Haya-suburi (also called *choyaku-shōmen-uchi*) is rapid *suburi*. It is difficult to comprehend the movement at first, and easy to fall into bad habits. *Haya-suburi* is just a fast version of a slow *men* strike with one major difference. That is, you do not go back to *chūdan* after the *men* strike. Every time you strike *men*, your hands go back overhead. Some people start *haya-suburi* from the *migi-jodan* position (hands above the head), and others start it from *chūdan*.

Haya-suburi learning procedure

1. Assume *chūdan* and wait for the command to start.

2. On the command, "*Yōi!* (ready)", lift your hands overhead.

3. On the command, "*Hajime!* (begin/start)", strike *men* stepping forward from the right foot.

4. Step back from the left foot while lifting your hands overhead again.

5. Repeat 3 and 4 until told to stop.

1. Take *chūdan*

2. *Yōi*

3. Stepping forwards to strike *men*

4. Step back and hands overhead

<u>**Command**</u>

1. *Haya-suburi*, "*Yoi*!"
2. "*Hajime*!"
3. *Ichi, Ni, San, Shi...Kyu, Ju*

4. Repeat the counting
5. "*Yame!*"

<u>*<Kiai>*</u>

Shout *men* after each count.

<u>Instructor</u>: *Haya suburi, Yōi, Hajime! Ichi!*

<u>Everyone</u>: *Men*

<u>Instructor</u>: *Ni!*

<u>Everyone</u>: *Men*

<u>Instructor</u>: *San!*

<u>Everyone</u>: *Men*

..

<u>Instructor</u>: *Kyu!*

<u>Everyone</u>: *Men*

<u>Instructor</u>: *Ju!*

<u>Everyone</u>: *Men*

..

<u>Instructor</u>: *Yame!*

<u>** Things you should keep in mind **</u>

Even though the strikes are executed rapidly, don't ignore the basics. Do it slowly at first making sure that your form is correct.

1. When striking *men*, do not leave your left foot behind (snap the left foot up as you cut).

2. Make sure that you are actually aiming to strike *men*, and not just swinging a stick.

3. When stepping back, do not leave your right foot in the air (this is very common). The right and the left foot always end up in the basic stance position.

Basic Stance

It is very important to learn *haya-suburi* correctly. This movement is very helpful to learn quick strikes.

COLUMN: FUMIKOMI = STOMPING?

Fumikomi is translated as "stomping", and probably because of this, many people try to just "stomp" without thinking about why we do it. Kick off with the left (back) foot and use the right foot to pull your body up and forward. There is another word, *fumikiri*, which is often confused with *fumikomi*. *Fumikiri* refers to the function of the back foot, and means "to kick off from the floor or ground in order to propel yourself forward". The right or left foot is used in the long jump to fling our bodies through the air. *Fumikiri* is basically the same action, so if the left foot is used to kick off the floor, it is the *fumikiri-ashi*.

As written in my online article "Why *fumikomi-ashi* in *kendo*?"[42], *fumikomi* is not utilised so much in traditional *kenjutsu*, but *fumikiri* certainly is. Many say *fumikomi* must be performed in *kendo*; otherwise, it is not *ki-ken-tai-itchi*. Others claim that the actual stomping part is not so important, as long as practitioners have good posture. In other words sliding forward with *suri-ashi* is sufficient as long as a practitioner shows good *zanshin*, *tenouchi* and *ki-ken-tai-itchi*. These are completely different views, but I support the latter line of thinking.

I have seen many people who started *kendo* in their later years, and have a difficult time mastering *fumikomi*. You must be patient as it takes time to learn this properly. Many 8-*dan* and 9-*dan sensei* do not do *fumikomi* because they are not capable of doing it anymore. Still, they are able to soundly defeat younger practitioners without even working up a sweat My point is that *fumikomi* comes as a result of "reaching from a distance, fast". As long as we deliver our body forward with a kick-off from the back foot with *ki-ken-tai-itchi*, "stomping" is not necessary. Concentrate on "propelling your body forward" rather than "stomping". That way, you will be able to maintain balance while executing the cut.

---

[42] http://www.kendo-guide.com/why-fumikomiashi-in-kendo.html

27. SUMMARY: TANDOKU-DŌSA

People tend to shy away from spending too much time learning the basic movements, *tandoku-dōsa*. If you cannot do these basic movements, you will never learn the more advanced techniques properly. People outside Japan like us have fewer opportunities to practice with good instructors. That means it is very hard to fix bad habits and improve.

All that you can do in this situation is to learn the basics correctly, and practice them over and over. If you are not in a good environment to learn *kendō*, you will have to work harder than those who are. The movements introduced in this book should be practiced constantly. Once you have mastered *san-kyodō* and *ni-kyodō*, move onto *ikkyodō*. *Kendō* is all about repetition. We repeat the same movements over and over for years. It can be boring, but it has to be done. In *kendō*, we need to persevere and never succumb to weaknesses such as stopping training because we are bored. We do not stop training because we get tired. Why? Because the whole point is to challenge and discipline ourselves.

Never skim over the basics. Do not think that you only have to do the basics when you are a beginner. The basics in *kendō* means a lot more. They are the lifeline of *kendō* as a lifelong course of study. If anything, I hope the book has made this last point crystal clear to those about to enter the world of *kendō*. Good things come to those who have the patience to continue.

Hiro Imafuji

Kendo-guide.Com

Kendo For Life, LLC

ABOUT THE AUTHOR

Masahiro "Hiro" Imafuji was born in 1973. He is the founder and representative of Kendo For Life, LLC and runs the website, Kendo-Guide.Com. Hiro started *kendō* at the age of 7 at *Shūbukan* in *Itami* City, *Hyōgo*, Japan. *Shūbukan* has more than 200 years of history and is counted as one of the three greatest privately owned *dojos* in Japan.

The *Shihan* (head master of the dojo) at that time was the late *Juichi Tsurumaru-sensei* (9-*dan*) who graduated from *Budo Senmon Gakko* (a pre-war national school for training young men to teach *kendō* and other martial arts). Hiro learned *kendō* from the late Tsurumaru-*sensei*, the late Murayama-*sensei* (8-*dan*) and Miyazaki-*sensei* (7-*dan*).

After spending six years in New Zealand teaching to local kendoists, he relocated to Guatemala and instructed Guatemalan kendoists between 2000 and 2002 as a full-time volunteer of Japan International Cooperation Agency and helped them to form an official *kendō* association.

Upon moving to the United States, he started instructing *kendō* at West Virginia University, and assisted in the formation of a *kendō* club in 2005. Currently, he instructs at Mudokwan and Gotokukan Imafuji Dojo in Indianapolis, Indiana. He holds the rank of 6-*dan* in *kendō*.

Printed in Great Britain
by Amazon